Brendan Behan's Island

By Brendan Behan

Borstal Boy
Brendan Behan's New York (with Paul Hogarth)
Hold Your Hour and Have Another
(with decorations by Beatrice Behan)

The Quare Fellow
The Hostage
The Big House

By Paul Hogarth

Defiant People: Drawings of Greece Today
Looking at China
The Face of Europe
People Like Us
Creative Pencil Drawing
Brendan Behan's New York (with Brendan Behan)
Majorca Observed (with Robert Graves)
London à la Mode (with Malcolm Muggeridge)
Artist as Reporter
Russian Journey (with A. Jacob)
Drawing People
Artists on Horseback
Drawing Architecture
Paul Hogarth's American Album
Creative Ink Drawing
Walking Tours of Old Philadelphia
Walking Tours of Old Boston
America Observed (with Stephen Spender
Arthur Boyd Houghton

Brendan Behan's Island

An Irish Sketch-book

BY

BRENDAN BEHAN

WITH DRAWINGS BY

PAUL HOGARTH

LITTLE, BROWN AND COMPANY
BOSTON   TORONTO

Library of Congress Cataloging in Publication Data

Behan, Brendan.
  Brendan Behan's island.

  Reprint. Originally published: London : Hutchinson, 1962.
    1. Behan, Brendan—Homes and haunts—Ireland.
  2. Ireland—Description and travel—1951–1980.
  3. Ireland—Social life and customs—20th century.
  4. Authors, Irish—20th century—Biography.
  I. Hogarth, Paul, 1917–   . II. Title.
  PR6003.E417Z4635 1985   822'.914 [B]   85-55
  ISBN 0-316-08776-9
  ISBN 0-316-08773-4 (pbk.)

PRINTED IN THE UNITED STATES OF AMERICA

Brendan Behan after the lobster

Contents

Acknowledgements

ACKNOWLEDGEMENTS are due to The Bodley Head, Ltd., for permission to quote from *Ulysses*, by James Joyce; M. H. Gill & Sons and Sceilg's executors for permission to quote from *Beatha Cathal Brugha* by Sceilg; MacGibbon & Kee, Ltd., for permission to reproduce the poem 'A Pint of Plain is your Only Man' from *At Swim-Two-Birds*, by Flann O'Brien; Christine, Countess of Longford, for the late Lord Longford's translation of *Lay Aside Your Arms* by Pierce Ferriter; Mrs. F. R. Higgins, for permission to use two stanzas from *The Gap of Brightness*, by F. R. Higgins; Maurice Craig, for his *Ballad to a Traditional Refrain*; Sean O'Riada, for permission to reproduce the song *As I Entered Down Wild Kerry*; 'Iascaire' for permission to use *As down the glen one Easter morn*; *The Standard, Envoy, New Statesman, Twentieth Century*, B.B.C., and Radio Eireann.

The English translations of my poems *The Blaskets, Thanks to James Joyce* and *Oscar Wilde* are by Valentin Iremonger, whom I should like to thank, together with Rae Jeffs, for valuable assistance and much patience.

Do mo Bh.

To Pat my wife
these drawings are dedicated.

. . . it is clear that for a stranger the Irish ways are the pleasantest, for here he is at once made happy and at home.

WILLIAM MAKEPEACE THACKERAY:

Irish Sketch Book

I

Dublin's Fair City

As DOWN THE GLEN one Easter morn to a city fair rode I,
There armed lines of marching men in squadrons passed me by.
No pipe did hum, no battle drum did sound its last tattoo
But the Angelus bell o'er the Liffey swell rang out in the foggy dew.

Right proudly high in Dublin town, they hung out the flag of war.
'Twas better to die 'neath an Irish sky than at Suvla or Sud-El-Bar.
And from the plains of Royal Meath, strong men came hurrying through
While Britannia's Huns, with their great big guns, sailed in with the foggy dew.

O, the night fell black and the rifles' crack made perfidious Albion reel.
'Mid the leaden rain, seven tongues of flame did shine o'er the lines of steel.
By each shining blade a prayer was said that to Ireland her sons would be true
And when morning broke, still the war flag shook its folds in the foggy dew.

But the bravest fell and the requiem bell rang mournfully and clear
For those who died that Eastertide in the springtime of the year;
While the world did gaze with deep amaze at those fearless men but few
Who bore the fight that Freedom's light might shine through the foggy dew.

Ah! back through the glen I rode again and my heart with grief was sore
For I parted then with valiant men whom I never shall see more;
But to and fro in my dreams I go, and I kneel and pray for you,
For slavery fled, O glorious dead, when you fell in the foggy dew.

Well, she saw a lot of trouble, Dublin; but not all her songs were, as
they say, of war and slaughter, Doran's ass and barrels of porter. They
also knew the heart-scald of men chasing women or, as happens now
and again during leap-year and the three years leading up to it, of
women chasing men:

I left me father, I left me mother,
I left me brothers and sisters too.
I left me friends and kind relations,
I left them all for to follow you.

For love is teasing, first hot, then freezing.
Love is a wonder when first got new;
But as it grows older, it soon grows colder,
And fades away like the morning dew.

Oh! love and porter make young men older
And love and whiskey make old men decay;
So what can't be cured, love, must be endured, love,
And so I am off to Americay,

Singing, ' Love is teasing, first hot, then freezing,
Love is a wonder when first got new;
But as it grows older, it soon grows colder,
And fades away with the morning dew.'

Well, that's a bit like the Scots song, *Waly, Waly, gin love be bonny*,
but you get songs like that, I suppose, common to every country.
When I was at school, we used to sing a version of *Lord Randal* that
went like this:

What'll you give your sister, Henery, me son,
What'll you give your sister, my pretty one?
Pizened be-ans,
Pizened be-ans;
Make my bed,
I've a pain in my head
And I want to lie down.

But, then, we said more nor our prayers in the slums of North
Dublin where I was born—less than an ass's roar from Nelson's
Pillar. I come from the same area as Sean O'Casey about whom I don't
intend to say anything for the simple reason that it would be like

O'Casey's Dublin. Mountjoy Square tenement

praising the Lakes of Killarney – a piece of impertinence. As far as I'm concerned, all I can say is that O'Casey's like champagne, one's wedding night, or the Aurora Borealis or whatever you call them – all them lights. At the time I was young, this area was pretty bad but that's one thing I must give the Government credit for – they built lovely flats for the people. You wouldn't see anything in Dublin now like the slum parts of Westbourne Park in London or some parts of Glasgow. Mind you, it was pretty bad while it lasted. I was born in a Georgian house that had gone to rack and ruin as a tenement, so I should know. It's been knocked down since but without any remorse on my part, much as I admire the Georgian Society whose activities are all right as long as they're confined to the houses of wealthy doctors in Fitzwilliam Street.

Lovely garden estates the Government built when they were clearing the slums but somehow the people hated leaving where they had been reared and where they had reared their children. They had a social status in their way in those slums that was destroyed altogether when they were shifted out to Crumlin or Kimmage and set down in terrace houses mixing with God knows what muck from Irishtown, Ringsend, the Liberties and other parts south of the Liffey. I remember, when we got our notice to get moving, hearing one oul' wan moaning to my mother: 'Oh! Mrs. Behing, jewel and darling! don't go out to Kimmage – that's where they ate their young.' Four miles away it was, and no more, where this cannibalism took place.

Not far away is Nelson Street where I happened to set the scene of *The Hostage*. Most of the incidents in that play were taken from life though, needless to say, I fiddled around a lot with them – catch me leaving anything unembroidered. The incident of the British Tommy occurred actually in Belfast but, in real life, I'm happy to say, he wasn't shot. As a matter of fact, he said later that he spent the best four days of his life in the hands of the I.R.A. He was captured at a place called Ballykinlar Camp in County Down. He wasn't taken as a hostage at all but he'd been around by accident when the I.R.A. were raiding the place for arms, so they brought him home with them for a while. They kept him in a house on the Falls Road in Belfast and he wasn't at all upset because he knew he wasn't going to be shot. The incident moved me and remained in my mind because I thought it was tragic for young fellows from England to be stuck in Northern Ireland – or any part of Ireland for that matter – but particularly in the North with their cute faces and their bowler hats. You might as well set any decent Tommy

The house in Nelson Street
where Brendan Behan set 'The Hostage'

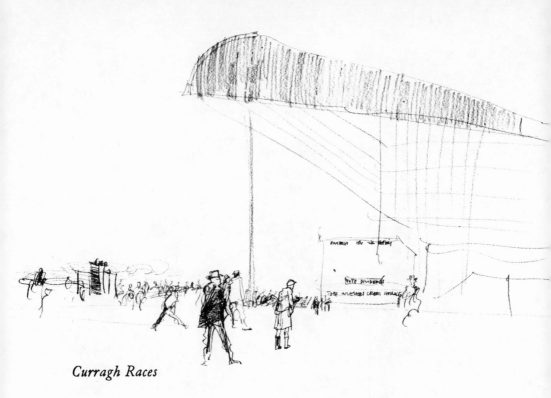

Curragh Races

down in the environs of the Stock Exchange in London – he'd die of fright.

At the back of my mind, too, was a story I heard from the leader of a Flying Column about something that happened during the War of Independence. A Flying Column, in case you don't know, was a full-time mobile section of the I.R.A. They lived in the hills and off the country and performed great feats from 1919 to 1921 and again in 1922 and 1923. This man told me how he found out about a train that was travelling from one place to another somewhere in County Kerry along a stretch of railway where there were no arches or no bridges. It was a warm summer's day and the troops – boys of seventeen and eighteen – sat out on top of the train as they went along. Suddenly they ran into my friend's ambush. He told me it was like as if they were on holiday. They were singing away and all of a sudden they found themselves in the midst of a war. At the time I heard this story, I thought it was tragic and I still think so. I mean, the fellows who shot them had nothing against them and they had nothing in particular against the people that were shooting them. But that's war. It's only the generals and the politicians that are actively interested in it.

I wrote the play very quickly – in about twelve days or so. I wrote it

Curragh Races

in Irish and it was first put on in Irish in Dublin. I saw the rehearsals of this version and while I admire the producer, Frank Dermody, tremendously, his idea of a play is not my idea of a play. I don't say that his is inferior to mine or that mine is inferior to his — it just so happens that I don't agree with him. He's of the school of Abbey Theatre naturalism of which I'm not a pupil. Joan Littlewood, I found, suited my requirements exactly. She has the same views on the theatre that I have, which is that the music hall is the thing to aim at for to amuse people and any time they get bored, divert them with a song or a dance. I've always thought T. S. Eliot wasn't far wrong when he said that the main problem of the dramatist today was to keep his audience amused; and that while they were laughing their heads off, you could be up to any bloody thing behind their backs; and it was what you were doing behind their bloody backs that made your play great.

But if I go on like this, I'll begin to think I'm getting above myself like the time I published a piece of verse in Irish in the *Irish Times*. It was about the death of Wilde in Paris. It was much praised by the local mandarins and later in the week there was a vicious letter in the paper attacking it as 'brutal and ugly'. Jesus help my wit, didn't I think I was a great man altogether when complete strangers would go to the trouble of abusing me, until I discovered that the letter was by someone who disliked me on grounds purely racial and social, and thought it a disgrace that the likes of me should be allowed into print at all unless it would be into the criminal intelligence.

I suppose they were great days – I was younger anyway – and even if I had no money there were people in the literary pubs in the vicinity of Grafton Street that would give me an odd pint of porter or a glass of malt betimes, as long as I could listen respectfully enough to the old chat about Angst. A generation or so ago they were arsing around the bog, and a bowl of stirabout and a couple of platefuls of spuds would have cured all the Angst from here back to Norway; but since the change-over in 1922, when they got well down to the porridge-pot, there was no holding them. It started off with top-hats and white ties and getting into the gentry and then to chatting about the servant problem with the Anglo-Irish Horse-Protestants (who at least were reared to it) and it went from that to late dinner and now it's Angst, no less.

Not that the Horse-Protestants were any better, but they were longer at it. They are just as ignorant except that their ill-manners are sharpened by time. Sheridan was a peasant's grandson, Yeats an artist's son, Wilde a doctor's son, Parnell was the grandson of an American sea-captain, Robert Emmet a doctor's son, Bernard Shaw a clerk. The myth of the Anglo-Irish, and the attempt to drag Irish writers (particularly those who happened to be Protestants) after the fox-hunt and the royalist inanity, would have us believe that the most rapacious rack-renting landlord-class in Europe were really lamps of culture in a bog of darkness, doing good by stealth and shoving copies of *Horizon* under the half-doors of the peasantry after dark and making wedding presents to the cottagers of Ganymede Press reproductions of Gauguin.

There is, of course, no such thing as an Anglo-Irishman, as Shaw pointed out in the preface to *John Bull's Other Island* – except as a class distinction. Even all Protestant genius is not nobbled for the stable-boys and girls. It must, at least, wear a collar and tie. Sean O'Casey is not claimed as an Anglo-Irish writer because he had no land except what a window-box would hold on the window-sill of a tenement. The Belfast industrial workers, who are the thickest concentration of royalism and pro-Britishism in Ireland, are never claimed as Anglo-Irish. The whole thing nowadays is a middle-class myth. One thing about Dublin which is indicative of this is that the middle classes are inflicted with a desire to ride. They have their daughters going bandy taking riding lessons out there in Stillorgan and competing at the Horse Show. When Yeats said about Dublin: 'Great hatred, little room,' he was referring to the middle and so-called upper classes. Joyce described the same crowd as 'the centre of paralysis'. John Mitchell, a rebel leader of 1848, was being transported to Van Diemen's Land and, passing in the ship the villas on Killiney Hill on the south side of the bay, he described it as 'a city of genteel dastards and bellowing slaves'. I remember once saying to my father: 'I suppose he really said bastards but they changed it to dastards for reasons of respectability.' 'No,' said my father, 'It's nobody's fault to be a bastard but to be a dastard you have to work at it.'

And the middle classes are that way to this very day. They will go to London and attend a play of mine or of Sean O'Casey's and they will inform all the English people that, of course, to really understand this play you've got to come from Dublin. Back at home, they will adopt either the straightforward outraged indignation of the censor and say: 'We think this is a disgusting and immoral play,' or they will say, as they have said about me, that I write to please English audiences – they'd stand on their hands to please any English audience themselves. Straightforward censorship is fairly harmless – no Irish writer is really injured by it. He is damaged by the indirect and unauthorized censorship which goes beyond the reasonable suppression of pornography. Some years ago, I was looking for a copy of Plato's *Symposium* when it appeared as a Penguin. I got it in the end but with a good deal of difficulty. The censorship could hardly get after him at this time of the day but, as one bookman (saving your presence) said to me: 'We saw a slight run on it, and the same sort of people looking for it, so we just took it out of circulation ourselves. After all, we don't have to be made decent-minded by Act of the Dail. We have our own way of detecting smut, no matter how ancient.'

It's the working class that binds me to this town; they're the only real people here. The middle classes put years on me. If they didn't see my name in the *Sunday Times* and the *Observer*, they wouldn't want to know me; and that goes for Catholics as well as Protestants, lawyers as well as doctors. Not that I'm idealizing the working class – far from it. They don't pretend to care. Their attitude is, well, they know me a long time, they've seen me around for as long as they can remember and they don't give a damn what I'm doing or think I'm doing. They've a great spirit and good neighbourly hearts – if they couldn't do you a good turn, well, they wouldn't do you a bad one.

You find the people I like on both sides of the river but, mainly, they live more or less along a line that you might draw between the Custom House and Glasnevin Cemetery – between birth and death, come to think of it. The Custom House is a remarkable building – though, to tell you the truth, I'm not particularly knowledgeable about architecture, Georgian or otherwise, possibly due to an architect friend solemnly informing me at some stage in a very austere voice: 'Good architecture is invisible.' The Custom House, as far as I'm concerned, is notable mainly for the fact that it was there I used to get false birth certificates in order to get false passports when I was in the I.R.A. It was burned by the Volunteers in 1921 and that's what brought British administration in Ireland finally to a standstill, for all local government records were housed there. Across the way from it stood Liberty Hall, the headquarters of the Irish Transport and General Workers' Union, where the Irish Citizen Army had its headquarters in 1916. It has been knocked down now and they're building a skyscraper block on the site.

Not far away is the General Post Office which was the headquarters of the 1916 Rising. The story of the Rising is too well known to go into it all again, but during that week an aunt of mine went down to the G.P.O. to look for her husband who was in there fighting. Shells from a gunboat on the Liffey were falling all around the place and my aunt was asked with some urgency to go away. (She had a baby son in her arms who was afterwards killed in France while fighting with the British Army in 1944.) She refused to get away and kept demanding to see her husband who finally came to a sandbagged window and roared: 'Go away, Maggie,' and she shouted back: 'I only wanted to know if you were going to your work in the morning.'

Turning down Bachelor's Walk at the Liffey by O'Connell Bridge where British troops fired on the people of Dublin in 1914, you come to the Metal Bridge or, as it is sometimes called, the Ha'penny Bridge. It's known as the Metal Bridge for the very obvious and unIrish reason that it's made of metal, but in my father's day it was better known as the Ha'penny Bridge because you had to pay a halfpenny toll to cross it. Further along there is the Four Courts where the Anti-Treaty forces dug in in 1922. I remember the man that was more or less second-in-command there told me that during the attack on the building, a young I.R.A. man from the country – a boy of seventeen or eighteen – was going up the stairs carrying the

The Custom House

Chancellor's large wig. 'Hey, where are you going with that?' he called and the boy answered: 'I'm only going to take the kettle off the fire.'

Near by is O'Meara's pub – the 'Irish House', though why it should be called that in Ireland, I don't know. I used to know the man that owned it – it has changed hands since; and I remember him principally for a few lines of poetry that he recited to me:

> 'Then Hoolihan hit Hannaghan and Hannaghan hit McGilligan
> And everyone hit anyone of whom he had a spite,
> And Larry Dwyer, the cripple, who was sitting doing nothing
> Got a kick that broke his jawbone for not indulging in the fight.'

A friend of mine painted that pub one time – Dinny Bowles, a very famous man – a signwriter he was and a very good one at that.

Pubs are dull enough places at any time though not so dull in Ireland as they are in England. I suppose I know most of them in Dublin and I'd rather have them than the pubs in London. I remember being in the 'Blue Lion' in Parnell Street one day and the owner said to me: 'You owe me ten shillings,' he said, 'you broke a glass the last time you were here.' 'God bless us and save us,' I said, 'it must have been a very

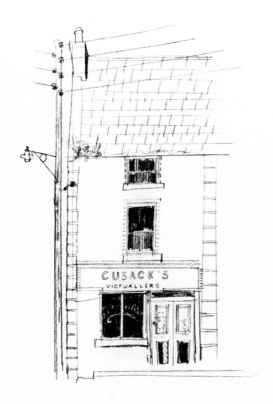

dear glass if it cost ten shillings. Tell us, was it a Waterford glass or something?' I discovered in double-quick time that it wasn't a glass that you'd drink out of he meant – it was a pane of glass and I'd stuck somebody's head through it.

It was about the Blue Lion also that I remember my grandmother, Christina, getting into a bit of embarrassment. It's more or less at the back of what was Joyce's Night-town, near Montgomery Street, which was one of the streets in the red light district. My grandmother had me by the hand and as we were walking down the street, we met a friend of hers who said: 'Come on, Christina, and have one', meaning come in for a glass of porter. So my grandmother said all right but she didn't want to go into the 'Blue Lion' because, she says: 'All those characters go in there' – meaning whores; but her friend says: 'Ah, they won't take any notice of us.' So in they went. 'We'll go in the private part,' she says and: 'All right,' says my grandmother. So when they went into the private part all the 'characters' roll up and say: 'Ah, hello, Christina, come on in, we didn't see you these years.'

There's a pub up near Guinness's Brewery on the Liffey Quay – it must be the nearest pub to Guinness's – known as 'The Shaky Man'.

I don't know if it's there now or not because it's a long time since I was in it, but I think it was there I heard one of my friends – a man named Crippen – refer to 'Evelyn Warr'. 'Aye', he said, 'Evelyn Warr was a tough woman.' I don't know what we had been talking about but I sang him a bar or two:

> 'They told me, Francis Hazley, they told me you were hung
> With red protruding eyeballs and black protruding tongue.'

And says he, 'Aye, Evelyn Warr,' he said, 'she was a great soldier and a great warrior. And she was called Evelyn because that was her name and she was called Warr because she was all for war.'

I was in 'The Shaky Man' one evening when a prostitute, who combined shoplifting with prostitution, came in and discovered that a pair of nylon knickers which she had carefully stolen from a Grafton Street shop that day, had disappeared during one of her absences on business. There was hell to pay, but all I remember of the row was her voice roaring again and again, in tones of the bitterest indignation: 'There's no honest whores left. There's no honest whores left.'

Or you'd have some old one sitting in the snug, where ladies who were ladies could have their jorums without the rude gazes of the men, and they'd remember Johnny going off in his pill-box cap to fight Kruger, or going off to do the Kaiser in, in the war after that. Like the time they were drawing the ring-money for their husbands away in the wars, one old one says to another:

'Anything in the paper this morning, Julia?'

'Nothing, Mary, only the Pope is trying to make peace.'

'God forgive him, it's a wonder he wouldn't mind his own interference. It's enough to make you turn Protestant.'

> Hand me down me petticoat, hand me down me shawl,
> Hand me down me petticoat for I'm off to the Linen Hall,
> *With your he was a quare one,*
> *Fol-de-do and g' ou' a that,*
> *He was a quare one, I tell you.*
>
> If you go to the Curragh camp, just ask for number nine,
> You'll see three swaddies standing there and the best looking one is mine.
>
> When he joined the Dublins, I know he gave a wrong name,
> And if I don't get me ring-money, it's his old one's all to blame.

My love is o'er the ocean, my love is o'er the say,
My love he is a darling chap and he left me in the family way.

And when they get across the say, out to fight the Boers,
Try and keep the Dublins back, see the Leinsters running before,
  With your he was a quare one
  Fol-de-do and g' ou' a that
  He was a quare one, I tell you.

Both the big Irish distilleries are not far from Guinness's – I suppose what makes both Irish whiskey and Guinness so good is the curative properties of Liffey water. Scotch whisky seems to be getting more popular than Irish now particularly in America. Its popularity there is due to the fact that Queen Victoria drank it. She didn't like the Irish and she wanted to be Celtic so she thought that maybe the Scots weren't so mad as the Irish and she became very Scots-minded. There were other influences on her too, I expect, but they didn't stop her exporting half the population of the Highlands to Canada. Irish whiskey is made in a pot-still, which is simply a pot surrounded by Irish anthracite coal from Kilkenny. Scotch whisky is made in a patent still which was invented by an Irishman named Angus Coffey who hawked it around the Irish distillers, who wouldn't have anything to do with him. So the Scots took it over and they made whisky in a series of pipes surrounded by peat, but now presumably heated by electricity. Most Scotch whiskies are blended, and a great number of them contain Irish whiskey which is exported for that purpose. The best Scotch whiskies are what are called 'single malt' which are not blended; they are straight whiskies and are very good indeed. The other Scotch whiskies I wouldn't give to a dog. The popularity of Scotch really only dates in these countries since the First War – never mind Victoria, she only influenced America which is slavishly royalty-minded. In Trollope's novels, for instance, when they're not scoffing claret in their clubs, they're knocking back Irish whiskey. It wouldn't surprise me at all to find Mr. Macmillan, who is an admirer of Trollope, I'm told, enjoying a quiet glass of Irish now and again for his health's sake. And if you ever look at that strip-cartoon in the *Daily Mail*, Flook, you'll find the conservative landed colonels dashing into their locals for a double Irish now and again. Only the lower classes drink Scotch; it sort of marks you off to go into a London pub and ask for Irish nowadays: when they've finished looking at you, they realise slowly that you've got a very eclectic palate.

Scotch, of course, is increasingly popular in Ireland, but that's because it's a bit dearer and the fact that you drink it indicates that you've got money – enough to pay for that ball of malt anyway. Most literary men go in for it now or for the glass of wine like Yeats. What's that he drank – not that he was ever seen in a pub– 'a glass of brimming Muscadel', I think, or maybe that was somebody else. My mother was a maid in the house owned by Madame Maud Gonne MacBride, and she knew Yeats quite well, but I never heard her advert to his drinking. He used to visit that house which was in St. Stephen's Green, and he used to call her 'Kitty' which she disliked for her name is Kathleen. He arranged his entrances to the house so infallibly that he was there just as she'd be coming up the stairs with a tray of tea and cakes and sandwiches for the visitors, and he'd stop and talk to her for a couple of minutes. I think it was probably an inverted form of snobbery to show the guests that he'd as leave talk to the housemaid as to a lord. But this didn't excuse my mother from Maud Gonne's tongue when she scolded her for having the tea cold.

My mother also told me that at lunch, where she often served Yeats, he was absolutely impervious to what he ate, as he didn't know what he was eating half the time. He absent-mindedly would put sugar in the soup and salt in the coffee and all sorts of peculiar things like that. The one dislike that he had in the way of food was parsnips. Once he was served parsnips by some mistake and he remarked: 'This is a very peculiar pudding.'

I was in the 'Deux Magots' in Paris one time and an American that I was introduced to asked me if I had known James Joyce. I said that I hadn't had that honour, but I told him that my mother had often served a meal to W. B. Yeats in Maud Gonne's house on Stephen's Green and that the poet turned up his nose to the parsnips. 'He didn't like parsnips?' said the American reaching for his notebook, 'You're sure this is factual?'

'It is to be hoped,' I replied, 'that you are not calling my mother a liar?'

'No, no, of course not,' he said, 'but she might have been mistaken – it might have been carrots,' he added hastily.

'You must think I'm a right fool to have a mother that can't tell a carrot from a parsnip.' I said nastily.

'No, no, of course – I mean I'm sure she could but it is very important. . . .' He wrote in the book: *Parsnips – attitude of Yeats to.*

Cleansing casks at Guinness's Brewery

'And you say he didn't like Stephen's Greens either – now what kind of vegetables are they?'

My wife also knew Maud Gonne MacBride very well in her old age. She used to visit occasionally at the house of Mrs. Stuart – wife of Francis Stuart, the novelist – down in Wicklow and she says that Maud Gonne retained her great spirit up to the time she died. Everybody that knew her, and plenty that knew her only to see, loved her. I remember her speaking at political meetings about prisoners in the thirties and even then she was a most magnificent figure – constantly smoking, she was practically a chain-smoker. One of her greatest friends was Madame Despard, a sister of French, a British general. She was an old suffragette with the Pankhursts and those in England. Madame Despard worked hard for Irish independence and was arrested in the twenties both by the British Government and by the Irish Government of the time. In 1932, I saw her at a tremendous meeting to greet the release of the political prisoners by the newly returned De Valera Government. Later that year, the priests in Dominick Street began preaching about Communism, and a mob of men marched up from a mission in Dominick Street Church to the workers' college which had been established by Madame Despard who by this time was a very old lady. They came up to set fire to the building but she thought they were a crowd come to greet her. She didn't know they'd come to burn her out. However, a few shots from the I.R.A., which at that time was a very anti-Fascist organization, soon dispersed the mob; it seemed to be favoured by the police, who didn't interfere with it.

Later Madame Despard retired to Ballycastle outside Belfast because she felt that the North would be the next place where the Irish Revolution would come to fruition. It's interesting to recall that the last time British troops were used in an Irish city against an Irish crowd was in Belfast in 1932 during the 'Outdoor Relief' riots. Crowds from both the Shankill Road, Sandy Row and the Falls Road marched together and converged on the City Hall and the fighting went on for three or four days. Protestant and Catholic fought together against the police and the military were brought in and fired on the crowd, killing two people. But the next year the Northern Government gave in to the rioters. The one thing they feared and still fear is the unity of the Catholic and Protestant worker. Two years later, the Orange leaders, by a series of inflammatory speeches, succeeded in starting what were known as the Jubilee Riots in which, to the intense satisfaction of the authorities, Catholic and Protestant once again fought each other rather than their common enemy, the police and the ruling class. But Madame Despard had always said – and I'm inclined to agree with her – that the next move in Irish revolutionary politics would be made by the Northern worker.

It was in the North that the first consciously organized Irish republican movement was formed. Outside Belfast there is a hill called Cave Hill, and it was on that hill that Theobald Wolfe Tone and a few friends took the oath and founded the United Irishmen. Tone was the greatest Irishman that ever lived and his autobiography is the seminal book of Irish radical republicanism. The United Irishmen were stronger in Belfast than anywhere else during his time, and Frank MacDermot points out in his biography of Tone that there was a very close connexion in the North between Freemasonry and the Republican organization – so much so that in 1797 and 1798 'a large proportion of Masonic lodges were practically revolutionary committees'. The bosses of the Masonic Order had to suspend its existence in 1798. It's a strange turn of fate that has the North today even more royalist-minded than the British middle classes.

Tone was himself a Dublinman and was born behind the Four Courts in what is now called Wolfe Tone Street. He was captured during the rebellion and was brought to Dublin and sentenced to death. As he was a soldier – a Chef de Brigade in the French Army – he asked that he should be shot but this was refused and he was condemned to be publicly hanged. On his last night in prison, he was mysteriously found dying – some say his gaolers had tried to kill him, some say he committed suicide rather than face the indignity, for a soldier, of hanging. He died that night anyway and he was waked near where he was born – in the Cornmarket. Although he is held in the utmost affection by every Irishman, the clergy have always been against him, and I remember some bishop referring to him as recently as 1934 or so as the 'cut-throat Tone'.

His autobiography makes great reading for he was a very human person with a great deal of affection and humour in his make-up. He liked his gargle, too, and makes no secret of the fact, and Frank MacDermot in his biography says that he was temperate by the general standard of the time and was never as footless as Pitt. He had a great smack for the people of his own city. He tells of how one day he was recruiting for France among captured British sailors, many of whom were press-ganged men from Ireland who were only too glad to throw over the King of England and to fight for the French. But one man didn't want to; and Tone tells: 'I heard a voice from the back in the accents of Ormond Quay call out impatiently, "If he won't enlist voluntarily and of his own free will, throw him in the wather, admiral."'

The area where Tone was born, and the area across the river immediately south, are two of the oldest parts of Dublin. They used to be the fashionable areas, but the opening of O'Connell Street, further down the river, drew the wealthier parts of the population down to the Georgian squares that were built about the same time – Merrion Square, Fitzwilliam Square, Parnell Square and the rest. South of the river, in the area I'm talking about, there is the old bastion of British rule in Ireland – Dublin Castle, in the dungeons of which so many died. Near by there is Christchurch Cathedral and St. Patrick's Cathedral where Dean Swift is buried. He was always a great defender of the Dublin poor. Behind the cathedrals, there are a few old-type markets; the principal one is the Daisy market. It's mainly a second-hand clothes market but it has other stuff too. I remember principally going through it one day and hearing a stall-holder remark: 'Keep the baby's bottom off the butter.' I've bought decanters there, very good ones, at a very cheap rate – I'm very fond of decanters, having a slight weakness for what goes into them. In the early thirties, when people still marched in great numbers to the First War Memorial at Island-bridge, soldiers used to repurchase their medals there – Mons stars, General Service Medals and indeed anything from the V.C. back-wards – for a small amount of money – and march into the Park wearing them.

There's another market over at Cole's Lane where I bought a massive chair which was carved from Burmese teak. I also bought a picture which hangs over my mantelpiece. It is of a bearded gentleman whom I give out is my grandfather though actually I don't know who the man is. There is also the Iveagh Market which is named after the Earl of Iveagh who gave the ground for it or something like that. The Guinness family have always been very good to the people of Dublin but as some wag remarked: 'The people of Dublin are very kind to the Guinnesses.' The Guinness Brewery at James's Gate is a huge place – almost a little town in itself. Although they have spread their wings very much in recent years, the fame of the Brewery still rests on its two traditional products – stout and porter. Porter is a lighter drink than stout and there's not all that much of it sold nowadays; but I recall my

A customer at the Daisy Market

father telling me that before the First War, when it cost a penny a pint, it was so good that the glass it was in used to stick to the counter. A friend of mine, Flann O'Brien, who wrote the brilliant novel *At Swim-Two-Birds*, has a little poem about it in that book; it's called *The Workman's Friend*:

When things go wrong and will not come right
Though you do the best you can,
When life looks black as the hours of night,
A pint of plain is your only man.

When money's tight and is hard to get
And your horse has also ran,
When all you have is a heap of debt
A pint of plain is your only man.

When health is bad and your heart feels strange
And your face is pale and wan,
When doctors say that you need a change
A pint of plain is your only man.

When food is scarce and your larder bare
And no rashers grease your pan,
When hunger grows as your meals grow rare
A pint of plain is your only man.

In time of trouble and lousy strife
You still have got a darling plan,
You still can turn to a brighter life
A pint of plain is your only man.

It's stout that is mostly drunk now, though both stout and porter have declined in quality since the last war. Somehow stout in Ireland is more palatable than the stout in London – they say it's the difference in the water. Guinness is, of course, universally drunk in Ireland and we are spared the extravagances of milk stout and oatmeal stout and the other proliferations of sweet stouts and ales.

Some of the Guinness family I know quite well – particularly Oona Guinness, now Mrs. Ferreras and formerly Lady Oranmore and Browne, and her two sons, Gareth and Tara. She lives at Luggala, a most beautiful estate in the heart of the Wicklow mountains. My wife and I usually spend Christmas there – among writers, artists, actors

Frank Crookes, cooper

and poets. Cyril Connolly was there one year in his red waistcoat and I sang rebel ballads for him the whole evening. He seemed to enjoy it.

Most of the Guinnesses live around Castleknock which is just on the far side of the Phoenix Park. This is one of the largest national parks in Europe. If you could imagine all the parks in Central London – from Kensington Gardens up to Hampstead Heath – put together, you'd have some idea of its size. It is less than two miles from the centre of the city and is very popular both in winter and summer. The President's residence is there as well as the American Embassy and the Apostolic Nunciature. I've spoken to the last President, Mr. Sean T. O Ceallaigh, but I can't say he ever asked me home even though he had been in gaol with my father in 1922 and 1923. The park is full of statues, mainly to British generals, and the I.R.A. spent a good deal of their time in the twenties and thirties trying to blow them up – a harmless enough occupation and a bit like their sentencing me to death one time in my absence: I sent them back a polite note saying that they could shoot me in my absence also.

It was in the Park that Lord Cavendish and Mr. Burke, both British Government officials, were killed in 1882 by the 'Invincibles'. The Invincibles were an extreme wing of the Fenians. I can't say that I ever felt much sorrow about the killings for, after all, Cavendish and Burke were imperialist agents in a country which hated them and didn't want them. The Invincibles were driven on that occasion by a character known as Skin-the-Goat. Where he got his name from I don't know. The Government offered Skin-the-Goat a thousand a year and a house in Canada if he'd give away on the men he drove, but 'No,' says Skin-the-Goat, James Fitzharris by name, 'I wasn't reared to the informing and you want to learn it off your mother to be much good at it.' So he went to Portland Prison for fifteen years instead and kept his mouth shut for the rest of his life. Except when someone would say 'the Park murders'. 'When was that?' Skin-the-Goat would say: 'I never heard of that. Oh, you mean the Invincibles? I drove the men right enough, but I drove no murderers, then or since.' One of the best songs I know is about Joe Brady who was one of the men executed for the killing:

> I am a bold undaunted youth, Joe Brady is my name.
> From the chapel of North Anne Street one Sunday as I came,
> All to my surprise who should I espy but Moreno and Cockade;*
> Says one unto the other: 'Here comes our Fenian blade.'
>
> * Detectives

I did not know the reason why they ordered me to stand.
I did not know the reason why they gave me such a command.
But when I saw James Carey there, I knew I was betrayed.
I'll face death before dishonour and die a Fenian blade.

They marched me up North Anne Street without the least delay.
The people passed me on the path, it filled them with dismay.
My sister cried: 'I'll see you, Joe, if old Mallon* gives me lave,
Keep up your heart for Ireland like a true-born Fenian Blade.'

It happened in the Phoenix Park all in the month of May.
Lord Cavendish and Burke came out for to see the polo play,
James Carey gave the signal and his handkerchief he waved,
Then he gave full information against our Fenian blades.

It was in Kilmainham Prison the Invincibles were hung.
Mrs. Kelly she stood there all in mourning for her son.
She threw back her shawl and said to all: 'Though he fills a lime-pit grave
My son was no informer and he died a Fenian blade.'

Well, men must fight and women must weep, as Sean O'Casey says,
but betweentimes they get born, marry, and die. The poor have the
cheek and the impudence to die on nothing and they get married on
very little — two three's to the Parkgate for an afternoon honeymoon
walk in the Hollow or a visit to the Zoological Gardens:

> I brought me mot up to the Zoo
> For to show her the lion and the kangaroo;
> There were he-males and she-males of each shade and hue
> Inside the Zoological gardens.
> I went up there on my honeymoon;
> We saw the giraffe and the hairy baboon,
> There were parrots and larks and two doves all a-cooing
> Inside the Zoological Gardens.

> *Trouble and strife, it is no lark,*
> *Dublin city is in the dark;*
> *You want to get out to the Phoenix Park*
> *And view the Zoological Gardens.*

* A detective

'Oh,' says she, 'me darling Jack,
I'd love a ride on the elephant's back,'
'If you don't ge' ou' a that, I'll give you such a crack
Up in the Zoological Gardens.'
As I went up by the old Parkgate,
The polisman was upon his bate
And tried to make love to me darling Kate
Inside the Zoological Gardens.

Trouble and strife, it is no lark,
Dublin city is in the dark;
You want to get out to the Phoenix Park
And view the Zoological Gardens.

'Don't drag me like that or you'll ruin me frock.'
If you don't hurry up, Dunphy's door will be locked,
I can hear the bells ringing for seven o'clock
Inside the Zoological Gardens.'
At Dunphy's corner the tram did stop
We were just in time to get in for a drop
And I kissed her for one of the real old stock
Outside the Zoological Gardens.

Trouble and strife, it is no lark,
Dublin city is in the dark;
You want to get out to the Phoenix Park
And view the Zoological Gardens.

Dunphy's is where the mourners stopped on their way back from poor
Paddy Dignam's funeral in Joyce's *Ulysses*. I've always liked the
story there about the two drunks that came out one evening to look
for the grave of a friend of theirs. 'They asked for Mulcahy of the
Coombe and were told where he was buried. After traipsing about in
the fog they found the grave, sure enough. One of the drunks spelt
out the name: Terence Mulcahy. The other drunk was blinding up
at a statue of Our Saviour the widow had got put up . . . and, after
blinking up at the sacred figure, "Not a bloody bit like the man," says
he: "that's not Mulcahy", says he, "whoever done it."'

I don't know many working writers in Ireland because there aren't
many. There are civil servants, spoiled priests waiting to be re-
habilitated, judges, ex-convicts, retired nuns and escaped agricultur-

alists who write: but these are only honorary screevenorai.* They write a bit now and again for the *Irish Times*, *The Month*, Messrs. Sheed and Ward, the merrier ex-Trotskyist magazines in America, and the Irish editions of the English Sunday papers. The older Irish writers spend more or less of their time in France or the U.S.A. I do see one diligent writer now and again, but she is a former military policeman and my prejudices do not run in that direction. There are a few seedy Anglo-Irish Old Statesmen who have tried London, but they are usually the grandchildren of imported bailiffs from the English Black Country and I am too snobbish to associate with them. They are desperate bores anyhow, running down England for tiresome reasons of history; instead of running down its discomforts, bad liquor, public houses without lavatories or telephones, and the fact that it is full of Irish, Welsh and Scots bogmen and English village idiots; and is dull except for a few vinous, elegant literary comedians and comediennes whose company is not readily available to the stranger.

You'll meet all our native writers, however, at the races — both horse and dog. There, at least, I must allow them a purer passion than the interest English Tory writers, bred in the hunting country of St. John's Wood, pretend in horse and hound. The Irish writer goes to the racing for the drink; and for outdoor drinking and intellectual conversation, it's hard to beat the dogs. Coursing is the best because you can stand in the tent and see the whole course without moving out at all.

I believe with Lenin that the main object of all political activity should be the abolition of the village idiot; and the inefficient attempts of two greyhounds to 'turn' a hare, which nearly always finishes in the hare being torn to bits, is sufficient excuse for me to retire to the whiskey tent and give myself an anaesthetic against the horrors and the screams outside.

I spent a day at a coursing meeting on the Boyne, with a priest of the Irish College in Paris who translated the verse of Paul Eluard, and saw him nod his head with a sad smile when someone remarked that a hare seldom lived more than a day or so after a course, even when he got through the escape and into his enclosure with the other refugees, from the shock to his nervous system. One of the honorary writers said they should have a psychiatrist for the hares on the other side and there was a general guffaw in which I joined. Not because I thought it was funny or because I approved of torturing clean fine beasts that did no more than nibble a piece of grass and sit peacefully on their forms in a

* Writers

Smithfield

field. I do not enjoy the track racing so much, not indeed that I miss the screams of the live hare, but there is less time for drinking and conversation and watching and listening to the honorary writers and overhearing their lying stories of high life in Paddington and the time they got drunk with the literary lady: '*Hey, shewer, as shewer as yewer settin there, May Deeditt turns rowend, hey, bedad, and she says, says she, "What matter about iz hevin the melodic line, if we hev the drink?" Hey, bedad, iz what she said.*'

At the track, one misses all this, and the only time an opportunity for conversation presented itself on the occasion of a track meeting, there were so many deathly pale countenances in the bar, among the real dog men, that we all, myself and the honorary writers, had to join in the long and bitter silence, broken only by the music and song coming from the track across the road:

> Sweet Heart of Jesus, we Thee implore,
> Oh, make us love Thee more and more. . . .

'Sweet Heart of Jesus,' muttered an elderly bookmaker, 'are they going to be there all night?' And added to the barman, with resignation, 'Bring us another, Mick.'

Behind Dame Street

I did not look even at May Deeditt's melodic china for the gloom and Angst at my own table would have done credit to Kafka, and any little quip on my part, about the time I dropped the *jeton* into Jean-Paul's *soupe de l'oignon* (being an urban and more travelled liar), would not have been well received.

This was an occasion when, in that bar, opposite Grangegorman Race Track, all and sundry sat in a deep and despairing gloom. At my own table, where I sat with the Owner, my hand shook as I raised my tumbler to my mouth. For this reason: our dog, which I shall call Molloy, was not thought much of against the favourite (called The Hero of Seventeen Ninety-Eight) and the Owner and myself had decided to have a coop about him, by causing him to run very quick indeed in this race, beat the opposition and make him win an awful lot of money for anyone with the foresight to bet on him with the book-makers some time before.

Now, I have experience about *stopping* dogs. I know nothing about horses, dogs or cabbages, except to look at or eat, but I had the privilege of working for, and still have the privilege of knowing, a London burglar and smuggler who did a very successful job of dog manipulation. A slum and under-privileged child like myself, he knew nothing of agriculture either, but with the simplicity of a corner boy, he got over a fence at a London track and removed a board from the back of two kennels, fed sausage rolls and saveloys to the occupants and then went out and backed the third and made a whole lot of money. He did this many times till they started building kennels back to back, surrounded by electric wire and lit up all night like a German concentration camp.

But here in Ireland there was a difference between a man stopping someone else's dog and giving something to his own to stimulate its running. It was often done, and once the beast was removed from the track without being taken over by the stewards and having his spit analysed, there was no danger. But in the case of the stewards having their suspicions aroused, not only was there a danger, but a positive certainty of a criminal charge against the trainer and the owner and a sentence of at least twelve Irish calendar months from the judge – and a longer sentence if it so happened that the judge had been at the track that night and had backed something else in the same race.

Now I had a doctor friend who frequently advised on matters of stimulation, and he had come from Liverpool (another city of doggery and boggery – poverty-stricken kips, every one of them) with a preparation used in heart cases that worked scientifically and accurately in stimulating the running of a greyhound if timed and measured in the proper quantity. He had frequently advised me on this matter.

This mixture was tried and found to be indeed the thing for making quick greyhounds quicker and it worked like magic. In the words of the poet, this dog Molloy would meet himself coming back, after the judicious injection. But one of its magic properties was that after it worked to its peak capacity, it was static for a moment or two and then began to work in the opposite direction, making the poor dog very tired.

That evening I called down and met the Kennelman who, by reason of being an old friend and by signing a piece of paper, agreed to let the Owner and myself transport the dog to the track to hand over to the authorities concerned.

'Go aisy with him, Brendan,' he said, 'and not a bite to eat nor a sup to drink, you understand.'

I sat with Molloy in the back of the car with a wrist-watch and, as the bells chimed the Angelus from the city churches in the distance, I raised the hypodermic needle, lifted the dog's right leg, pressed the needle into the great vein, lowered the dog's leg and said: 'That's that.' It was twenty miles to the track and we were to leave in our entries with the kennelmen at the track one hour before the first race, which was at eight o'clock.

Molloy was in the second race at eight-fifteen and his dose was scientifically measured to put him in peak speed at that time. He would continue to be very lively for a while after that till he could be collected with the winnings and brought home. Fifteen minutes it would take until he got drowsy and sleepy, falling finally into a deep coma from which the noise of a hydrogen bomb or a Redemptorist preacher would not wake him. By that time, we figured he would be safely tucked up in the back of the car, bowling home on the rocky road to Dublin.

We started off in great form and went out through the Phoenix Park, which is especially lovely on an April evening where you can see the deer in the distance and maybe the first of the squirrels, and fellows and girls locked together in the long grass and giggling and squirming, and taking no notice whatever of the Lenten Regulations, which in our diocese, ordain that there shall be no mixed laughing during the seven weeks.

As we came out on the Chapelizod Road, past that place on the Liffey's banks where Tristan and Iseult rested awhile, if you can call it resting, and not far from that other spot notorious to all culture vultures, under the Magazine Wall, where Humpty Dumpty had a great fall in *Finnegan's Wake* by the Rev. Seamus O'Seoighe,* S.J., (ret.). And all passed off very civil in our motor-car, with Molloy there sitting up at the back with his little cover over his middle and panting away there like a whore on duty – which is a known thing that if the slowest greyhound in the known world saved his breath and became a total abstainer from panting and licking, he would save that much energy that he could look back and shout 'come on' to a cheetah instead of, as happened when the matter was put to the test, the cheetah jumping impatiently over the greyhound to get home.

The next thing I'm looking up at a banner spread across the road which reads: 'God Bless Our Lord.'

I chuckled, a thing I don't remember having done before, and went to say something but the owner looks round from the front seat and putting up a warning finger says: 'Nark it, Brendan, nark it.

---

* James Joyce.

It is not a lucky thing to mock religion and we going out to do a stroke.'

I subsided; and we came to another one which read: 'Grangegorman Stands By The Rosary.'

Ah, 'twas then I fell in. There was this priest from Hollywood, America (I do not say America from affectation as if none of us had heard of Hollywood before – some of my best friends are Hollywoodians – but there is also Hollywood, County Wicklow and Holywood, County Down and I've a reason for making this clear) and he was preaching what they called a Rosary Crusade and had been received with great rallies like Billy Graham all over the big cities of the States – Boston, New York, Philly, Chi., L.A., etc. – and in London where, now I come to think of it, he held a huge rally at Olympia; but for some reason he had never held a meeting in Dublin. Many of the faithful wondered why this was, and some made out it was because the ecclesiastical authorities here did not like his technique; and now there was this little town of Grangegorman giving us in Dublin the rub – that they, the people of Grangegorman, stood by the Rosary whatever the big city free-thinkers and/or the narrow-minded Jansenists might do.

As we came nearer the town, it was obvious that they were having a big rally that very night and, as we approached the dog-track, I laughed – but fearsomely and with covert glances at my unsuspecting companion in the front seat and with sympathy at poor old Molloy beside me. There was bunting and flags and little altars, and all that lively grandeur of an Irish religious festival that give bad Catholics like myself the totally unearned satisfaction that ours is the church of Raphael and Leonardo and, indeed, as I remarked to the late Hannen Swaffer when he told me he was a spiritualist, we keep a better type of ghost.

'Listen,' I said, 'I think they're holding a Rosary rally——'

'Look here,' said the Owner, 'it's no skin off your nose what they're holding.'

We came nearer the track and the bunting was intensified and a big banner left over from the Eucharistic Congress of 1932 was stretched across the avenue leading to the gate. It showed St. Patrick with green whiskers and a big fat snake the width of a porter-barrel trailing after him and under it was written, '*Fáilte, a Thighearna, um Cháisc*' which means, 'Welcome, O Lord, at Easter' – only the fellow had made a mistake in his Irish and had written '*Fáilte, a Thighearna, um Cháise*' which made it read: 'Welcome, O Lord, at cheese'; but I said nothing about that but only tried to warn the Owner: 'But they're holding the rally at ——.'

'Listen now, and for Jesus sake and for the last time, it's all bloody equal to you where they bloody well hold their bloody rally. They're not interfering with you, and they're not asking you to go to it, and you know what these country people are. I suppose you want to get us run out of this kip the way you got us run out of Belcuddy the time you started arguing the toss about Ireland being sold to the English by Nicholas ——stick that you said was a Pope.'

'Nicholas Breakspear.'

'Nicholas any ——ing thing you like. Didn't the man prove to you there was no Pope called Nicholas any ——ing thing, and now you're trying to get us pitched out of this place.'

'I'm only trying to tell you that this Rosary rally is being held in ——'.

The Owner turned and roared at me: 'I don't care a fiddler's ——k where it's being held.' Then he softened and said: 'Now keep easy, for Jesus' good sake, till I hand this dog over at the track here.'

I sighed and held my peace and we went down and he was a pleasure to see, making the other old bowelers look like an advertisement for Bile Beans if I didn't know what I knew.

The chap at the kennels took the dog, wrote in his book and looked up: 'Yous know, of course, about the Rosary rally, men?'

The Owner smiled ingratiatingly and said: 'Ah, yes, a great thing, too. I mean I'm not over-religious myself, God forgive me ——.'

The kennelman nodded soothingly: 'Er-em-yes-er-em-we-all-shure-er-en-err . . .'

'But it's a great thing all the same. A man all the way from America.'

'Ah, yes,' says the kennelman, 'shure we told the priest when he asked for the loan of the track; "The dog men," says we, "the dog men, they may take an ould jar and that."'

'True,' said the Owner, owning up to it, 'It's true for you.'

'"And sure", we told him, "they may have their faults but there's not one of them will begrudge you the track for such a good purpose." And after all,' he turned to us, 'it only means putting racing back for an hour and a half.'

'What?' asked the Owner.

'They'll only have the track for an hour, and all the races are put back until it's cleared.'

He nodded and went towards the gate without saying anything with me following. As he let us out, the kennelman said, 'I suppose you can kill an hour in the hotel opposite,' and he smiled and added, 'some of the dog men are going to pass the time even better – by coming to the rally.'

We went into the hotel and the Owner, always a fair man, said: 'One glass of whiskey and a glass of gin and tonic.' The gin was for me for I had spent some of my time among the Anglo-Irish of Scotland Road, Liverpool.

'I can see us eating an awful lot of porridge,' said the Owner, 'when they find that dog asleep in the kennels at racing time. Twelve ——ing months. . . .'

I went out during the rally when they had really got down to the business – praying hard, fervent whispers coming from thousands of voices in the dark. The Owner looked crazily at his malt when I came back a short while later half-dragging the dog and beckoning him out urgently.

'Into the car, for Christ's sake,' I roared and off we got.

'I went to the kennels and told the kennelman that the dog would start barking at a quarter-past eight and start all the other bloody dogs barking too. The bastard gave out that it would be against the rules of the Greyhound Association to hand out the dog till after the race, but I told him he thought more of his Greyhound Association than he did of the Catholic Church, and that I wasn't going to stand for an unseemly disturbance during a solemn part of the Benediction, and that I'd complain to the American priest about him. So he gave me the dog and I'm to bring him back when the rally is over.'

'Thanks be to the good Lord Jesus,' said the Owner, fervently, and crossed himself and said: 'Amen.'

We stopped at numerous pubs on the way home and I was permitted and, indeed, if I may say so, encouraged to sing several blasphemous songs.

But our poor oul' slob of a hound, fast and all as he might be with the help of the few jabs or a couple of pellets, was nothing compared to the fastest greyhound that ever lived – Master Magrath, stuffed now in Kensington Museum (and would to God that we were too):

> The hare she led on with a wonderful view,
> And swift as the wind o'er the green field she flew.
> But he jumped on her back and he held up his paw—
> 'Three cheers for old Ireland,' says Master McGrath.

[45]

The Metal (or Ha'penny) Bridge

The Four Courts

Sunday morning in the Bird Market

Dublin children in St. George's Place,
off Mountjoy Square

The Quay near Guinness's Brewery

A regular at the 'Blue Lion'

The Irish Derby at the Curragh

The Daisy Market

At the 'Blue Lion':
   Mary and Joe Cullen, together for 25 years

Mary Daly

Jerry White, cooper at Power's Distillery

A ROSNER

A Woman of No Standing

'AND THE PRIEST turns round to me' says Ria, 'and says he: "But you don't mean to say that this person still goes down to see him?"'

'"I do, Father."'

'"And brings him cigarettes?"'

'"Not now, Father, not cigarettes, he's gone past smoking and well past it, but a drop of chicken soup, tho' he can't manage that either, these last few days."'

'"Well, chicken soup or cigarettes," says the priest, "what really matters is that this person continues to visit him – continues to trouble his conscience – continues as a walking occasion of sin to stand between him and heaven. These Pigeon House people must be, shall be, told straight away. They'll be informed that you, and you only, are his lawfully wedded wife, and that she is only – what she is. Anyway, this way or that, into that sanatorium she goes no more."'

'You know,' puts in Máire, when Ria had finished, 'it's a known thing and a very well-known thing, that a person cannot die while there's something not settled in his conscience. That one going to see him so, outside of the insult to Mammy here, his lawful wife, not to mind me, his only daughter, for all we're away from him since I was five – on the top of all that she was doing his soul the height of injury, not to mind holding his body in a ferment of pain, below on this earth, down in that Pigeon House.'

'But no matter,' says Ria, 'the priest wasn't long about seeing the Reverend Mother and leaving strict instructions that she wasn't to be let in any more – that she was no more his lawful wedded wife than the holy nun herself.'

'So now,' said Máire, 'if you don't go down early tomorrow you'll not see him at all, because I doubt if his struggling spirit will back

[57]

away from Judgement any more, now that all is settled, and his mind at ease.'

He was still alive when I got down to the Pigeon House but she wasn't far out, because he didn't last out the night.

His face all caved in, and his hair that was once so brown and curly was matted in sweat, and God knows what colour.

Ah, you'd pity him all right, for the ruined remains of what was once the gassest little ex-Dublin Fusilier in the street – off with the belt and who began it – up the Toughs, Throttle the Turks, and Hell blast Gallipoli.

Ria, his wife, was the kindest woman in Ireland, and (I've heard my mother say) in her day, the best looking.

He died that night and the nun and Ria and Máire were charmed that he'd no mortal sin on his soul to detain him in torment for any longer than a few short years of harmonious torture in Purgatory.

The priest was delighted too, because, as he said: 'It's not when you die, but how you die that matters.'

As for the woman, no one saw her to know what she thought of it, but the priest gave strict orders that she wasn't to be let near the funeral.

The funeral was on the day after. He'd lain the night before in the mortuary chapel. They've a mortuary chapel in the Pigeon House sanatorium, nice and handy, and most soothing, I'm sure, to new patients coming in, it being close by the entrance gate.

There used to be an old scribble on the porch that said: 'Let all who enter here, leave hope behind.' But some hard chaw had the beatings of that and wrote: 'It's only a step from Killarney to heaven – come here and take the lift – any lung, chum?'

We had a few prayers that night, but she never turned up, and I was sorry, because to tell the truth, I was curious to see her.

At the funeral next day, our cars (Ria did it in style all right, whatever lingering scald her heart might hold for him) greased off the wet Pigeon House Road, through Ringsend, and into Pearse Street, and still no sign of her. Right up the Northside, and all the way to Glasnevin, and she never appeared.

Ria had the hearse go round the block where we'd all lived years ago – happy, healthy, though riotous betimes – fighting being better than loneliness.

I thought she'd have ambushed us here, but she didn't.

I had some idea of a big car (owned by a new and tolerant admirer) sweeping into the cortège from some side street or another, or else a cab that'd slide in, a woman in rich mourning heavily veiled in its corner.

But between the Pigeon House and the grave not a one came near us.

The sods were thrown in and all, and the grave diggers well away to it when Máire spotted her.

'Mother, get the full of your eyes of that one.'

'Where, *alanna?*' asks Ria.

'There,' said Máire, pointing towards a tree behind us. I looked towards it.

All I could see was a poor middle-aged woman, bent in haggard prayer, dressed in the cast-off hat and coat of some flahool* old one she'd be doing a day's work for (maybe not so flahool* either, for sometimes they'll stop a day's pay on the head of some old rag, rejected from a jumble sale).

'But I thought,' says I to Ria, 'that she'd be like – like – that she'd be dolled up to the nines – paint and powder and a fur coat maybe.'

'Fur coat, how are you,' said Ria scornfully, 'and she out scrubbing halls for me dear departed this last four years – since he took bad.'

She went off from behind her tree before we left the cemetery.

When Ria, Máire and myself got into the Brian Boru, there she was at the end of the counter.

I called two drinks and a mineral for Máire, and as soon as she heard my voice, she looked up, finished her gill of plain porter and went off.

She passed quite near us and she going out the door – her head down and a pale hunted look in her eyes.

* *Flaitheamhal:* Gaelic for 'generous'

Biddy Kelly at the 'Blue Lion'

John Laflin, Dublin art student

James Relph,
for 37 years a cooper

Guinness's Brewery

MANHATTAN PEANUTS

A trio at Slattery's

The Three Fates, at Slattery's

The Rock of Cashel

2

The Warm South

By Killarney's lakes and fells,
Emerald isles and winding bays,
Mountain paths and woodland dells
Beauty ever fondly strays. . . .

IT'S NOT A GOOD POEM – or even a very good song, to my mind –
but it's the only one I know about Killarney, which for all its beauty
is more or less unsung for the simple reason that even an ad-man
would be ashamed to attempt to eulogize it. There are many famous
things and many famous experiences in this life that disappoint people,
but there are two things that did not disappoint me – my first taste of
champagne and my first look at the Lakes of Killarney. It's as elusive
to try to remember the feeling of your first look at it as to try to recall
the smell of the hair of the girl you first kissed – but you keep trying.
Apart from that, though, I remember Killarney mostly for the great
variety of the pubs and the immeasurable hospitality of the hotels
which tourism has never spoiled. The best way to come to it is from
West Cork and around by the coast doing what is called the Ring of
Kerry.

I worked in this area once – in Caherdaniel – on the pious task of
trying to restore Daniel O'Connell's old home. He's by way of being a
saint now in Ireland, but that didn't make the shop-keepers put their
hands in their pockets, between their visits to Lough Derg and
Croagh Patrick, to help on the work, and the old house is still there
falling into rack and ruin, if I may coin a phrase.

Near by, at one part of a very lonely road overlooking the bay, there
was a shooting – about twenty years ago – and the police came down in
droves but couldn't find out anything about it. So one policeman
dressed as a tinker, and he went to an old lady living beside the house

in which the shooting took place. The shot must have nearly deafened her.

'Would you give me some hot water,' he said, 'for to make a cup of tea, if you please?' Which she did and they carried on a conversation in Irish. During the talking, he said to her: 'I'm a tinker', which aroused her suspicions immediately for tinkers, as a rule, don't speak Irish – but as she hadn't very much English he had to speak Irish to her. He talked about the weather, the crops and one thing and another and 'Tell us,' he said, 'wasn't that a terrible thing that happened up in the house yonder when the man was shot?'

'Oh,' says she, 'I never heard anything of that', though, as I say, the shot must have deafened her barring her being deaf already which she didn't seem to be. So he asked her a lot of questions and to each one of them she answered she didn't know, she didn't know.

'Tell me, ma'am,' says he, 'do you know anything?' And he pointed out over the Atlantic Ocean to the Blasket Islands lying out in the bay and he said, 'Tell me, ma'am,' he says, 'do you know the names of those three islands out there?'

'I couldn't tell you, sir,' she said, 'They weren't there when I'd gone to bed last night.'

The same Blasket Islands form the last points of Europe before America. Up to 1946 or so there were still families living on the biggest island – not getting much of a living, as far as we call it living, but contented enough with the little they could get from the few sheep they could keep. Three books – good ones – came out of this small community of a few hundred people. One of them entitled simply *Peig* was by one of the oldest of the islanders, Peig Sayers. She was married to a man of English descent – how people with names like Sayers and Perkins and Piggott got to these outlandish places I don't know, except that the English must be as good at travelling to strange places as the Irish. Peig, in fact, wrote two books, but perhaps the two books from the Blaskets best known are: *The Islandman* and *Twenty Years A-Growing*. The first is by Tomás Ó Criomhthain and was translated into English by Robin Flower, a Keeper in the British Museum, who himself wrote two of the best books ever written about Ireland: *The Irish Tradition* and *The Western Island*. The other was written by Maurice O'Sullivan, a policeman (if I have to say a good word for him myself) which also appeared in Penguins, some years ago. All three are dead now, the Lord have mercy on them, because as O Criomhthain said, we shall not look upon their like again. Nobody

*Off the Dingle Peninsula:
the Blasket Islands*

lives on the islands now; they have all been moved to the mainland with the help of Government grants and the like, but nobody can say if they're any way happier or not.

Years ago, when the last inhabitants of the Blaskets were moved to the mainland, I was lying on what passed for a bed in Mountjoy Jail in Dublin doing fourteen years. I thought of the wonderful kind people they were and the free and independent, if frugal, lives they and their ancestors had on those islands, their eras of quiet happiness there on the uttermost fringe of Europe, and I wrote, in Irish, a poem lamenting the death of the islands. In translation, it goes roughly like this:

> The great sea under the sun will lie like a mirror,
> Not a boat sailing, not a living sign from a sinner,
> The golden eagle aloft in the distance the last
> Vestige of life by the ruined abandoned Blaskets.
>
> The sun will be gone, the shadow of night spreading
> As the moon, rising, through a cloud coldly stretches
> Its ghostly fingers over the silent earth
> Where, wracked, the shells of the houses stand deserted
>
> — Silent save for the birds all homeward flying
> Glad to be back, their heads on their breasts lying,
> And the wind soughing, softly a half-door swinging
> By cold wet hearths, their fires forever extinguished.

The Dingle Peninsula is still one of the places where Irish is spoken as the everyday language of the people and even then, it's only on the far tip of the peninsula. You get the older people, though, still coming in to Dingle who have nothing but Irish and, of course, some of the pub-keepers there make it their business to know what they are being asked for. Kerry Irish is a bit different from what they speak in the West Galway or Donegal areas — though not any more different than the German they speak in Prussia is different from what they speak in Bavaria; and God knows what Zomerzet man would understand a word out of a Yorkshire man's mouth, lavin' aside, your honour, the varieties of English spoken in Scotland or Wales, which as the world and his mother knows, are outlandish enough for anyone's lifetime.

One of the simplest examples I can give of the difference between the dialects is, indeed, the name of the language itself. Anglicized, the name of the Irish language is Gaelic; but it is only in Donegal that you will find the pronunciation remotely approaching that anglicized version. In Donegal, they say Gahlic — more or less as the word is pronounced in Scots Gaelic. In Galway and the West, they say: Gaylge; but in the south they say: Gayling. The word, in fact, is spelt Gaeilg, which pronounced at its face value would be Gaylig, leaving aside for the moment that even the consonants have values different from what they have in English: the English, God love them, expect every language to be like their own.

The Dingle Peninsula is one of the most beautiful parts of Ireland — long silver strands deserted even in high summer, and I hope it remains that way, though the tourist people seem determined to turn the place into a kind of English south coast. Ballyferriter, the last village before America, is a place I know well with its four good pubs resting snugly under the shadow of Mount Brandon or, if I may say so with proprietary pride, Brendan's Mountain — named from St. Brendan the mariner who is said to have discovered America about five or six hundred years before Columbus. A very decent and civil people, the Ballyferriter people — I remember one year being in a pub there late at night, during the time when the old licensing laws obtained. The pubs were supposed to shut at half past ten but, if you had travelled more than three miles — to have your pint among that kind congenial company — you were entitled to have the benefit of the *bona fide* provisions of the law up to midnight. None of us there that night lived further than a mile away, I need hardly say. At about eleven o'clock, the barman asked us if we'd mind moving outside and up the mountain a bit, as the police had sent word that they intended to carry out a raid at about a quarter past eleven. The barman, having replenished our glasses, led us out the back door and told us to go on up about a couple of hundred yards, and not to make too much noise while we were out there, as it would only upset the police if they had to take any action against either proprietor or patrons. It was a lovely starlit night and warm, too; and one of my most cherished recollections is of sitting out there on the side of Mount Brandon, looking at the mountain opposite called the Three Sisters framed against the clear moonlit sky and the quiet shimmering Atlantic, a pint of the creamiest Guinness in my hand as I conversed in quiet Irish with a couple of local farmers. After about three-quarters of an hour, the police having finished their business, the barman came out and beckoned us back and, with the relaxation of the nervous strain we had undergone, what could we do but sing until two o'clock or so — the memorable haunting

[71]

Cork Quay

Kerry landscape

Irish songs of the area, to which I was coaxed into adding a number of my own native songs from Russell Street, Dublin.

Further west than Ballyferriter is Dunquin, famous for the guest-house of the legendary 'Kruger' Kavanagh, the friend of many Hollywood film-stars, various American gangsters, boxers, politicians and similar sporting personalities. The late Monsignor 'Paddy' Browne, President of University College, Galway, until his death a couple of years ago, used to stay all summer in a bungalow near by, which now, I think, is owned by his niece, Máire MacEntee, daughter of Ireland's Deputy Prime Minister and now married to Conor Cruise O'Brien. 'Paddy' Browne was a mathematician but he also was a fine Irish-speaker and scholar, and translated many classical Greek plays into Irish as well as Dante's *Divine Comedy*.

On the way back into Dingle itself, you pass a ruined castle known as Ferriter's Castle. It was the home of the Ferriter family of whom the most famous was Pierce Ferriter. This was one of these Norman families that became more Irish than the Irish themselves, and when the rising of 1641 took place, Pierce took the Irish side. Throughout all these Cromwellian wars, he fought bravely and well and was indeed the last to surrender – which he did not do until 1653 when, despite the terms under which he capitulated, he was instantly hanged. He was also a poet and a lot of his poems survive. In many ways, he was like the Cavalier poets of the time, though he wrote out of an Irish tradition of Court poetry that was old when Boadicea was young. One of the poems of his I like best is available in the late Lord Longford's translation:

I charge you, lady, young and fair, straightaway to lay your arms aside.
Lay by your armour – would you dare to spread the slaughter far and wide?
O lady, lay your armour by, conceal your curling hair also,
For never was a man could fly the coils that o'er your bosom flow.

And if you answer, lady fair, that north or south you ne'er took life
Your very eyes, your glance, your air can murder without axe or knife.
And O if you but bare your knee, if you your soft hand's palm advance,
You'll slaughter many a company – what more is done with shield or lance?

O hide your bosom limey-white, your naked side conceal from me
And show them not in all men's sight, your breasts more bright than flowering
    tree.
And if in you there's shame or fear for all the murders you have done,
Let those bright eyes no more appear, those shining teeth be seen of none.

Lady, we tremble far and near, be with these conquests satisfied,
Unless they perish, lady dear, O lay those arms of yours aside.

Pierce Ferriter's aristocratic and intellectual mind could surmount
the tribulations of the time, but a more naturally vindictive note
appears in the general poetic remains of a period when Lord Mountjoy, Queen Elizabeth's Deputy, had laid waste the whole of Munster
so that not a crop grew in the whole province for many years. I've
always liked two epigrams in particular which belong roughly to that
period – the authors, of course being unknown. I give them in Máire
MacEntee's translations:

    I. May we never taste of death nor quit this vale of tears
        Until we see the Englishry go begging down the years,
        Packs on their backs to earn a penny pay,
        In little leaking boots, as we did in our day.

    II. Time has o'erthrown, the wind has blown away
        Alastair, Caesar, such great names as they –
        See Troy and Tara where in grass they lie –
        Even the very English might yet die!

And, while I'm on the subject, I'm reminded of the priest who, in
recent years, was in the habit of devoting his Sunday sermons to the
iniquities of pagan and immoral England. Sunday after Sunday, he
denounced the stew-pots of London, Birmingham, Manchester,
Liverpool, until at last the Bishop had to intervene because most of the
parishioners had sons and daughters over there, working hard and
sending home good money; but the parents were beginning to get
very worried about the whole position. The priest was instructed to
lay off England and, of course, he had no option but to obey. The
following Sunday, he chose to speak on the Last Supper and he
recounted the events that led up to the evening of Holy Thursday.
'And the Lord,' said the priest, leaning intently over the pulpit,
'said to His Apostles gathered there, "One who is at this table will
betray me", and as He said this, His eye rested momentarily on Judas.
Judas started and, with his hands trembling, said to His Lord: "Cor
blimey, guv'nor, turn it up. I ain't goin' to knock you."'
Things, of course, die hard in people's memories, and betrayal
looms very large in the history of England's government of Ireland.
The city of Limerick is north of Kerry on the Shannon and was sub-

jected to a long seige during the Williamite wars. In the end, although the citizens stood their hardships very bravely – I think because they had to – a treaty was concluded between the two sides; but the ink was hardly dry on the paper before every article of the treaty was broken by the English authorities, and the most onerous Penal Laws enforced against Catholics all over Ireland. Maybe it's the race-memory of that broken treaty that had Limerick such a fervently Catholic city, for, apart from its ham, its main claim to fame is that it has a huge Catholic Confraternity which is said to comprise over ninety per cent of the city's population. The Confraternity, besides being very large, is also very enthusiastic, and they hold a Mission every Lent at which, for a week, a priest comes and preaches to them about their sins, and they have prayers and Benediction every night lasting for hours, but ending before closing time. On the final Sunday, they go to Mass and Holy Communion in the morning, and in the evening there is a final service at which the congregation renew their baptismal vows. So every man gets a candle and takes it with him to the church and, at the appropriate time, the priest tells them to light their candles. It's a marvellous sight – and I say it quite genuinely and sincerely – to see these thousands of candles all lighting up the cathedral. Anyhow, they hold up their candles and the priest calls upon them to renounce the devil and all his works and pomps and they all say, 'We do'.

'Louder,' says the priest, 'louder and scare away the devil and all his works and pomps.'

As one man they shouted, 'We do'.

'Louder still,' said the priest, 'let him hear you in hell or wherever he is. Do you renounce the devil with all his works and pomps?'

'We do', shouted the congregation, and one very enthusiastic member roared: 'We do, we do, the dirty bastard.'

There was one famous member of the Limerickmen's Confraternity known as the Daddy Crowe who accompanied the group on a pilgrimage to Rome. They were all received in audience by the Pope, and at the end of the audience each member went up to the throne, took the Pope's hand and kissed his ring. But the Daddy Crowe didn't merely kiss his ring – he took him by the hand, shook it heartily and said: 'Jasus, Holy Father, there's not a man in Limerick that wouldn't go to hell for you.'

Taking a girl out in Limerick, as you might guess, has its difficulties. 'O Limerick girls are beautiful as everybody knows' as the song has it, but they're also very careful about keeping their legs shut, if not their mouths. A boy who takes a girl out in Limerick gives her tea, brings her to a picture or a dance, treats her to a drink or something at the dance, and some supper afterwards. Then he asks can he bring her home. He takes her to the gate of her house, puts his arm around her and she says breathlessly: 'Goodnight now it's nearly twelve o'clock. Jasus I'll be kilt thanks for everything,' and she's gone.

And sure, there's no harm in it at all. Down on the Limerick-Cork border, there was a sturdy farmer of about forty years of age who suddenly, to his parish priest's dismay, upped and married a Protestant lady from the Palatinate in the county. However, the priest was agreeably surprised when, after three months of marriage, the wife came along to him and asked for instruction in the Faith. In due course, she was received into the Church and the couple lived happily together until her death about seven or eight years later. After a couple of years of widowhood, the farmer, to the priest's horror, married another Protestant lady, but again the priest was overjoyed when she, in turn, came along after a few months of marriage and was received into the Church. She too died about ten years later and the farmer again was left alone in the world. After a year, he entered the bonds of wedlock again and for the third time to a Protestant lady. The parish priest made no fuss about the matter this time seeing that the two previous wives had ended up in no time as good-living devout Catholics. The third wife, however, showed no hurry in going down to the parish priest and, by the end of a year, he began to get worried. Up he goes to the farm and sees the farmer.

'What's the meaning of this, John?' says the parish priest, 'your wife hasn't come near me since you were married. It's a shame for you, John, and you after giving such good example for the whole county by converting your previous wives. What on earth is the matter at all?'

John, who was by this time well past sixty, sat there dejectedly in the chair looking at the parish priest. 'Ah! Father,' says he sadly, 'sure, the oul' convertor isn't what it was!'

Well, it's not all that far from Blarney where the famous castle is and the stone that all the tourists kiss. I've never seen a native of Blarney kissing the stone – I suppose they don't have to. I was in a public-house, the Blarney Tavern, one time with my brother and some cousins, and some old men came in wearing tweed suits of a type known as 'Martin Henry' suits. One of them called for a drink for himself and his friends and they spoke in very low and soft Cork accents. One man produced a roll of notes, thick enough to choke a bull, and even if they were only single notes, there must have been up to a hundred in the wad. He peeled off one, took his change, took up his drink and resumed his conversation with his friends.

My brother called the proprietor to one side and said; 'That man, if you don't mind me saying so, although he looks poorly dressed, is obviously carrying an awful lot of money. Who is he and who are they?'

'Oh,' said the proprietor, 'those are poor men from the asylum come out for a drink.'

'Well,' said my brother, 'I often heard that the Cork people were clever but if a lunatic can go around with fifty or sixty pounds stuck in his coat, what must the sane people be like?'

But Blarney I remember best for a very strange poem about it. It's called *The Groves of Blarney* and they say that Garibaldi's soldiers sang it as a marching song on some of their expeditions. I'm not surprised, knowing what soldiers are like; but it does leave me somewhat taken aback that it's included in every Irish school anthology:

> The groves of Blarney
> They look so charming
> Down by the purling
>   Of sweet silent brooks,
> Being banked with posies
> That spontaneous grow there
> Planted in order
>   By the sweet rock close.
> 'Tis there's the daisy
> And the sweet carnation,
> The blooming pink
>   And the rose so fair,
> The daffydowndilly,
> Likewise the lily,
> All flowers that scent
>   The sweet, fragrant air.
>
> 'Tis Lady Jeffers
> That owns this station;
> Like Alexander
>   Or Queen Helen fair.
> There's no commander
> In all the nation,
> For emulation
>   Can with her compare.

Such walls surround her
That no nine-pounder
Could dare to plunder
   Her place of strength;
But Oliver Cromwell
Her he did pommell
And made a breach
   In her battlement.

There's gravel walks there
For speculation
And conversation
   In sweet solitude.
'Tis there the lover
May hear the dove, or
The gentle plover
   In the afternoon;
And if a lady
Would be so engaging
As to walk alone in
   Those shady bowers,
'Tis there the courtier
He may transport her
Into some fort, or
   All underground.

For 'tis there's a cave where
No daylight enters,
But cats and badgers
   Are forever bred;
Being mossed by nature,
That makes it sweeter
Than a coach-and-six or
   A feather bed.
'Tis there the lake is
Well stored with perches
And comely eels in
   The verdant mud;
Beside the leeches
And groves of beeches,
Standing in order
   For to guard the flood.

There's statues gracing
This noble place in –
All heathen gods
   And nymphs so fair;
Bold Neptune, Plutarch,
And Nicodemus
All standing naked
   In the open air.
So now to finish
This brave narration,
Which my poor genii
   Could not entwine;
But were I Homer
Or Nebuchadnezzar,
'Tis in every feature
   I would make it shine.

And they say that sex is only in its infancy in Ireland! That was written about the beginning of the nineteenth century by Richard Milliken, an artist and musician; and if he'd like to be the courtier up above there, I can't say I'd mind it either. I think it was around this area of West Cork that the musician, Seán Ó Riada, collected a very strange song that I once heard the poet, Thomas Kinsella, singing. It has a very strange melody in the traditional mode:

As I entered down wild Kerry
With a seven-foot revolver in my right hand
I shot him off the ladder
Just the same as you'd shoot a crow.

Right in the middle of the great Atlantic ocean
There grows a plum-tree
And 'tis I haves the notion
'Twas the cause of the separation
'Twixt my true love and me.

Cork city itself is one of the most thriving cities in these islands and in recent years has become a very wealthy place where the people get up before their breakfast. Nice kind decent people, every one of them and, if I say it myself, there's no truth in the Dublin saying that when a Corkman starts calling you 'oul' son', it's too late to look for the

Cork: Coal Quay Market

knife in your back. The focal point of Cork is Shandon, the church bells of which are to a Corkman what Bow Bells are to Londoners:

With deep affection
And recollection
I often think of
    Those Shandon bells,
Whose sound so wild would,
In the days of childhood,
Fling round my cradle
    Their magic spells.

On this I ponder
Where'er I wander,
And thus grow fonder,
    Sweet Cork of thee,
With thy bells of Shandon
That sound so grand on
The pleasant waters
    Of the river Lee.

It's a Protestant church, of course, but the song was written by a Jesuit and I expect he knew what he was doing, though probably the late Bishop of Cork wouldn't agree with him. The story is told that the late Bishop, the Most Reverend Doctor Daniel Cohalan — known affectionately to all Cork people as 'Danny Boy' — lay in his last illness. He was very old — he must have been about ninety-four when he died — and his illness dragged on and on. What happened but the Protestant Bishop of Cork, a very much younger man, upped and died before him. The Monsignori brought the news to 'Danny Boy' and stood around waiting for the words of spiritual consolation that they would convey to the Protestant chapter. There was a long silence. After two or three minutes, 'Danny Boy' opened an eye, looked at the Monsignori and said to them: 'Well, he knows now who's the Bishop of Cork!'

Down from Shandon, there's a place called the Coal Quay where the feather-pluckers operate. These are ladies that pluck the feathers off geese and turkeys for the Christmas market, and indeed, during the rest of the year, their livelihood is got from plucking chickens. From time to time like the rest of us, they have been known to fall out occasionally on a Friday or a Saturday night and have a few words. One of them appeared before the District Justice on a Monday morning on a charge of having had a row with a colleague the previous Saturday, and the Judge says to her, 'What's your occupation?'

So she says: 'Your Worship, I'm a feather-plucker.'

'I know you are, my good woman,' says the Judge, 'but what do you work at?'

As I said, it's a very affluent city, Cork, with a good reputation for work, and it was there that Henry Ford in 1920 established their first European factory. Some time thereabouts the Cork Brigade of the I.R.A. were conducting some operations against the British that necessitated the use of motor transport – lorries – which the Brigade didn't have. Fords, of course, had plenty, so a few of the I.R.A. went down and held up the staff and the manager and demanded some lorries in the name of the Irish Republic.

The manager of the works, being a very clever and quick-thinking man, announced, 'I'm sorry,' he said, 'you can't have any in the name of the Irish Republic because these works,' he said, 'are the property of a citizen of the United States of America with which the Irish Republic is not at war.'

But the commanding officer of the I.R.A. was what the times demanded of him, a quicker-thinking man, and he turned away and wrote something on a piece of paper. He turned back to the manager and, 'Here,' he said, 'read that.'

And the manager read out: 'In the name of the Irish Republic, I solemnly do as from this moment declare war on the United States of America.'

'Now,' says the commanding officer, 'hand over them bloody lorries quick.'

There was another famous commander in Cork during that time also, who was noted for his personal bravery and excellent organization during the War of Independence. Many years later, during the Second World War, when in Ireland the showing of war news-reels from either side was prohibited, he heard that there was a news-reel of a British General surrendering; and he asked the manager to let him see it. The manager arranged a private showing after the ordinary show for himself and a few personal friends and the manager asked the former guerilla commander why he wanted to see it.

'Well,' said the commandant, for such he was, 'the same General, when he was a major in 1920, surrendered to me, and' he continued, 'I'd like to see him surrendering again.'

So the film was shown and they saw the General handing over his sword to an enemy officer who took it from him. When the film was over, they said to the commandant, 'When he surrendered to you did he hand you his sword?'

'Yes,' he said, 'he did, and I flung it in the ditch.'

'You must have been very bitter against the British,' they said.

'No,' said the commandant, 'it wasn't so much that, for I soldiered with the Tommies up to 1918; but I hated officers.'

One of Cork's most famous sons is Seamus Murphy, a sculptor of genius. I visited him once when he was in hospital. It was at the end of a bus ride outside Cork city and it was a rather dark winter's night as I got off the bus and started to turn into the drive leading to the hospital. I could hear a number of probationer nurses or wardsmaids – young girls anyway as I could hear from their laughter – in the bushes with a few boys.

As I turned and looked up the drive, I saw two nuns coming towards me so I shouted, 'Quick, here's two nuns', and they, no doubt grateful for my warning, scattered. But though I'd noticed the nuns, what I hadn't noticed was a huge Franciscan friar standing behind me.

He gripped me by the back of the neck and roared, 'What do you mean by that?'

'What do I mean by what?' I said; 'Unhand me, sir' – for I can be very verbose at times.

'Shouting,' says he, 'into those ones about the nuns coming down.'

'Well,' I said, 'it's none of your business, is it?' – my judgement getting the better of me again. 'I don't know what you mean,' I said, 'I didn't shout anything into them,' and I denied that it was I that shouted, though there wasn't anyone else within an ass's roar of the place.

The friar went up to the two nuns and said: 'Those girls of yours were in there in the bushes with boys, and this man here shouted in to them and gave warning of your approach. But I had my eye on them the whole time and I was waiting on you to come down for I knew you'd be coming down to catch them.'

'Oh! no,' said the nuns, 'we didn't come down to catch anybody. We came down to meet a man called Brendan Behan who's coming to visit Seamus Murphy and we knew he'd be on this bus' – and I was escorted in state up the drive.

During the course of my visit, it came to Seamus's brandy time, so the nuns produced the bottle of Hennessy and they gave Seamus his treatment which consisted of a glass of brandy; and they decided that,

Muckross Abbey

as I was there too, I might as well have some treatment also. I must be one of the very few people to have been treated to a couple of glasses of brandy by a nun!

It was somewhere in this area that the couple lived that, to their great disappointment, had had no children in all their years of marriage. They prayed and they went on pilgrimages and in the end, I'm glad to say, they were finally blessed with a son. It was such a miraculous event that they decided the boy would have to have a very special name, so after discussing the question for a long time they called the child Jesus. So Jesus Maloney grew up, a fine healthy boy, and off he goes to school where he does very well and his masters are proud of him. As a reward for doing so nicely in his examinations, they decided to bring him, as a treat, to Rome where the school choir was about to visit and sing before the Pope. The great day came, the choir sang beautifully before the Pope, and when they were finished, the Pope came down to them and walked along talking to the boys and shaking hands with them, and they all kissed his ring. Suddenly the Pope stopped and pointed to a boy who was sitting very demurely and quietly on a chair towards the back of the choir.

'Who is that boy?' said the Pope, 'why is he sitting down?'

'Jesus Maloney don't sing,' said the teacher.

'Christ,' said the Pope, 'he could stand up!'

Anyway, this is the area that Michael Collins, perhaps the greatest of Irish revolutionary leaders, came from. 'A fine big handsome young man he was,' my mother told me a thousand times, 'and if he had money to give to the wife, or the mother of a prisoner, or a man on the run, or the family of one of the boys killed or wounded, shot or hanged, he would deliver it himself. The other head ones were very serious men, but we wives and mothers called Mick the laughing boy.'

'I stand for an Irish civilization,' said Collins himself, 'based on the people and embodying the things – their habits, ways of thought, customs – that make them different – the sort of life that I was brought up in. . . . Once, years ago, a crowd of us were walking along the Shepherd's Bush Road when out of a lane came a chap with a donkey – just the sort of donkey and just the sort of cart they have at home. He came out quite suddenly and abruptly and we all cheered him. Nobody who has not been an exile will understand me, but I stand for that.'

Nearly forty years after the death of Collins and the execution of Erskine Childers by Collins's men, the Gaeltacht has declined by over one-third, and there are less native speakers of Irish than ever. The largest annual spiritual retreat conducted in the Irish language is given at St. Patrick's Church in Huddersfield. There are Gaelic football and hurling teams that have given up the game because most of the young men of the parish are in England or America.

Some time ago in the Dail, a Minister defended the purchase of a £50,000 estate in County Carlow by an English syndicate. There were landless men there, hoping to get small farms out of it so that they could stay at home. The Minister said that the Proclamation of the Republic guaranteed equal rights to all citizens and he could not take over the estate or discriminate against the Englishmen with the fifty thousand. Maybe he was acting in a more revolutionary spirit than he realized and future revolutionaries on that particular estate will not be confronted by troublesome sturdy small proprietors. Collective farming may begin immediately. In the meantime, the Carlowmen can go on over to England and spend the hours between three and seven p.m. on Sundays, hanging round the Shepherd's Bush Road, or the Edgware Road or King's Cross or Bayswater in the hopes of a consoling look at a donkey and cart.

If only Jim Larkin had learnt Irish – or Collins had studied Leninism! The connexion between them is closer than you may know. The Soviet Government had close contacts with the Irish Republican representatives in America and was the first country to recognize the thirty-two-county Republic of Ireland; just as the Republican Government and Parliament were, so far as I know, the first to recognize the Soviet Government in 1919. The Imperial Crown Jewels of the Romanoffs, or whatever the hell they called themselves when that show was on the road, lay for many years in the vaults of Government Buildings in Dublin, having been pawned as security for a loan given by the Irish Republic to the Soviet Republic in 1920. The Rising of 1916, in which Michael Collins fought bravely, was defended by Lenin when other socialists described it as 'a putsch.'

'Of the science of politics, we know nothing,' remarked Collins to Peadar Kearney, a brother of my mother's, author of the National Anthem and member of the Supreme Council of the Irish Republican Brotherhood. If Ireland now has less people and, naturally, less of 'their habits, ways of thought, customs' than she had in 1922, this is not what Michael Collins lived and worked for. It goes to show that if you want to make a revolution, it's as well to go and learn something about politics.

[87]

By politics, I do not mean, of course, the tactics of the pitch-and-toss school spiv, Birkenhead: or the earnest strivings of Lloyd George, the boy from the valley hoping to get on in the big smoke – the poor industrious old mug, trying to act the worldly and cynical, the Dull Old Thing, England's foreign-born lackey; and his lackey's lackey, Tom Jones, C.H., and much good it did him. How much nobler their countryman, Dylan Thomas, with his splendid statement: 'A job is death without dignity.' And by a job, Dylan Thomas – who was a very hard-working man – did not, of course, mean 'work'.

Nor by politics do I mean the tweedy frugalities of Eamon de Valera. Of course, I know that he was a brave man too, in his day. I had the melancholy experience of overhearing one of his executions by shooting during the war. I couldn't very well help it; it happened within a hundred yards of me and it seems that all the rifles were loaded.

Collins and Griffith allowed themselves to be tricked into Partition at the Treaty negotiations. Griffith worked all his life for Ireland's cause as he thought best. He thought the 1913 strike was unpatriotic because Murphy and the other industrialists were Irish employers. He did protest against the atrocities of the Dublin Metropolitan Police against the tenement dwellers: this was because they were an English force; and they were indeed founded by an ancestor of the Duke of Edinburgh, Prince Max of Battenburg, whose other claim to fame is that he licensed brothels and organized prostitution in the district made famous by James Joyce as 'Night-town.'

Collins and Griffith were innocent men and honourable men. Collins was a brave man, a kind man, and one of the greatest guerilla tacticians that ever lived. Collins, Griffith and de Valera accomplished many things. Three of them are: the hydro-electric schemes, the Turf* Development Board (perhaps the most successful outside Russia) and the housing revolution – particularly in the country areas where most families have a two-storied house with electricity and running water and far better facilities than the people in some parts of East Anglia, for instance.

But 'of the science of politics, we knew nothing'. If they had, the Irish would have been home and dried forty years ago instead of hanging round West London as they do today trying to get a look at an ass and cart.

To give the full rounded flavour of Collins's personality, perhaps

* 'Peat' in England

[88]

Ross Castle

the best book is by his fellow-Corkman, Frank O'Connor, who although
he fought against Collins after the Treaty, never lost his admiration
for, as he entitled his book, *The Big Fellow*. Another good book with
much later information is *Michael Collins,* by Rex Taylor, an Englishman but none the worse for that. Taylor had access, through his own
persistent efforts in tracking people down, to more information than
O'Connor, and his book contains four accounts of how Collins met
his death. There is another first-hand account given by Sceilg in *Beatha
Cathal Brugha* which Mr. Taylor couldn't be blamed for missing
because it is in Irish. I translate:

'There was a small band of I.R.A. men waiting at a cross-roads
expecting that Collins's band would come back in that direction.
After a good while, they went off in the direction they thought it,
now, more probable the other band would travel. Collins's party
approached sooner than expected. They had a scout out in front and
he heard the sound of a shot. He went back to give the alarm and
the armoured cars almost collided. There was a ditch running parallel
to this road, the width of a field away. There was a Volunteer (I.R.A.
man) behind this ditch, one man only; there were single trees
growing here and there along the ditch; the Volunteer fired a shot at
the cars from the cover of a tree; he ran forward in the cover of the

ditch firing one or two shots from the cover of the tree nearest to him and so forth. With that, and the armoured cars halted, a man jumped out and ran along the road, firing as he ran. The I.R.A. man in the cover of the tree aimed his gun again. "He is a brave man anyway," said he as he fired a bullet at him. With that, he saw the brave man raising up his own gun soft and easily over his head till he made a half-circle with it to fall on his side, dead. It was Michael Collins. After a while, the armoured car came back and they took his body in.'

Bernard Shaw wrote to Collins's sister:

'Don't let them make you miserable about it; how could a born soldier die better than at the victorious end of a good fight, falling to the shot of another Irishman – a damn fool but all the same an Irishman who thought he was fighting for Ireland–"A Roman to a Roman"? ... Tear up your mourning and hang up your brightest colours in his honour and let us all praise God that he had not to die in a stuffy bed of a trumpery cough, weakened by age and saddened by the disappointments that would have attended his work had he lived.'

After his death, the Irish made no song about him. Here, then, is one, *The Death of Michael Collins at Beal na mBlath* (the gap or mouth of flowers, the name of the valley he died in):

'Twas on an August morning, all in the dawning hours,
I went to take the warming air, all in the Mouth of Flowers,
And there I saw a maiden, and mournful was her cry,
'Ah, what will mend my broken heart, I've lost my Laughing Boy.'

'So strong, so wide and brave he was, I'll mourn his loss too sore,
When thinking that I'll hear the laugh or springing step no more,
Ah, curse the times, and sad the loss my heart to crucify,
That an Irish son with a rebel gun shot down my Laughing Boy.'

'Oh, had he died by Pearse's side or in the G.P.O.,
Killed by an English bullet from the rifle of the foe,
Or forcibly fed with Ashe lay dead in the dungeons of Mountjoy,
I'd have cried with pride for the way he died, my own dear Laughing Boy.'

'My princely love, can ageless love do more than tell to you,
Go raibh mile maith agat,* for all you tried to do,
For all you did, and would have done, my enemies to destroy,
I'll mourn your name and praise your fame, forever, my Laughing Boy.'

* A thousand thanks to you.

The Big House

THE BIG HOUSE (*Intones, slowly, majestically*): My bullocks, oh, my bullocks. My bullocks, my beeves, sheep, in flocks, in herds, they surround me. My people, too, in the ghosts of their generations. Old Baldcock built me. Three hundred years ago. Released from the stocks at Bristol on condition that he come to Ireland and assist in the civilizing of this unhappy isle, he came and made a thriving business, swindling Cromwell's soldiery out of their grants of land. If old Baldcock did not win it by the sword, well he did a better thing. He won it off them that did win it by the sword. Those that live by the sword shall perish by the . . .

A most tremendous explosion is heard.

MRS. BALDCOCK (*She leaps up in bed*): Ananias! (*Screeches*) Ananias! Ananias! Wake up! We're blown up! Blow up! I mean, wake up!

ANANIAS BALDCOCK: Yes, yes, damn it, Boadicea, I'm woken up.

MRS. BALDCOCK: I shan't stand it a moment longer. I knew we'd be blown up.

ANANIAS: We haven't been blown up. Damn it, we're still here in bed. That explosion was a mile away.

MRS. BALDCOCK: Well you might have some sympathy for whoever's house it was that was blown up. Not that it was anyone that matters, I suppose. There is no country house left in the neighbourhood for miles around. Hoggitts, Blood-Gores, Ramsbottoms, Snowteses, Pug-Footes, Grimeses . . . all the aristocratic names, all the grace and splendour and civilized living that the very syllables of those noble names recall . . . all . . . (*She sighs*) . . . gone away.

ANANIAS: There is nobody left in the district worth blowing up.

MRS. BALDCOCK (*Sadly*): I'm afraid you're right, Ananias. As a matter of fact (*more happy*) it can only have been the Civic Guard barracks.

ANANIAS: Maybe some of them have been killed ... or horribly mangled.

MRS. BALDCOCK: At the risk of seeming bloody-minded, I'd say it's just as well to keep the Irish occupied in killing each other rather than in killing us.

ANANIAS: You forget, Boadicea, that I am Irish. Like my ancestors before me, I was born here.

MRS. BALDCOCK: If an ass is born in a stable, does that make it a horse?

ANANIAS: You forget, too, that most of the new Civic Guard are merely the old Royal Irish Constabulary with their cap-badges changed. Men who served their King and Country faithfully; and collaborated openly and defiantly in the North-East, and discreetly but efficiently in the South and West.

MRS. BALDCOCK: Well, serve them right for joining the rebels in the end and working for the Free State.

ANANIAS: You don't understand, Boadicea, that the Free State is the surest and best way of beating the rebels. Even Lord Birkenhead says so. 'Doing England's work, with an economy of English lives', he describes it.

LOONEY: Mashter, sir, and Mishtress, Mashter, sir, and Mishtress, Mashter, sir.

Other voices ... the heavy accents of the Civic Guards are heard.

SERGEANT: Tell them 'tis only till morning. Just a bit of a refuge for the night is all we want.

LOONEY: I will, sergeant, I will surely. (*Knocking on door*) Mashter, sir, and Mishtress.

MRS. BALDCOCK (*Exasperated*): There's old Looney at the door. What can he want?

ANANIAS: Dionysius O'Looney is a loyal old sort. They have been butlers here since the house was built. For three hundred years, as long as the Baldcocks have lived here, there has always been a Looney in Tonesollock House. They have.... (*Knocks again*).

LOONEY: Mashter, sir, and Mishtress....

MRS. BALDCOCK: Never mind his sterling qualities now. Ask him what he wants.

ANANIAS: What is it, Looney?

LOONEY: The Eye Orr Ah is after letting off a bum, sir.

ANANIAS: I know, I know, we heard it. But it wasn't anywhere near here.

[94]

LOONEY: No, sir, 'twas only the Guards' barracks, sir, and Mashter sir. . . .

SERGEANT: Tell them 'tis only till the morning.

LOONEY: Yes, sergeant. (*Louder*) And Mashter, sir, and Mishtress, the sergeant wants to know if we can put him up for the night. They've no place to go till morning.

SERGEANT: 'Tis only till morning, your honour, and we could shake down any ould place that'd be a shelter for us out of the wet, till we get the telephone going to Dublin in the morning.

ANANIAS: Very well. You can use the loft or one of the grooms' places.

SERGEANT: Thanks, sir, and a bed in heaven to you, sir.

ANANIAS: The same to you, my good fellow.

SERGEANT: And a bed in heaven to your good lady too, and good night, ma'm. We only wants a shakedown in the straw. (*They move off and his voice fades*) . . . sure what's wrong with us sleeping in straw. Wasn't Our Lord born in it?

MRS. BALDCOCK: They can have the whole of Tonesollock House for me. Ananias!

ANANIAS (*Tired*): Yes, Boadicea?

MRS. BALDCOCK: I've been in this horrible country twenty years too long . . . but not a day longer. I'm going to Hereward and Tabitha in Ealing. A dull, London suburb but peaceful, without guns and bombs going off every night for five years . . . and Ealing is private . . . without the native militia coming as refugees to live with one. Irish hospitality, I suppose. But I've had enough of it. Ananias, you can please yourself. If you love Tonesollock more than you love me, you'll. . . .

ANANIAS: I love you the most, Boadicea.

MRS. BALDCOCK: Very well then. We'll go together. You go in tomorrow to your solicitors. He'll find an agent and send in the rents, such as they are, and the proceeds of all cattle sales, and we leave directly for England. . . .

LOONEY (*Having shown the Sergeant and Guard to their accommodation*): There yous are now, Sergeant dear, and Guard. It's where the Protestant minister sleeps when he comes here. Himself and the wife, in that very bed. He's a Protestant of course, but a very religious man. The moans and groans of him there, kneeling there on that very floor when he's saying his night prayers would go through you.

SERGEANT (*Feeling the mattress*): Sure, that's a grand bed, Mr. Looney.

GUARD: We're very thankful to you, Mister Looney, to put up us two poor homeless wanderers.

SERGEANT: Aye, indeed, we are so, Mister Looney.

LOONEY: Is there anything more I could do for yous, now? Would you like a drop of anything to restore your shattered nerves?

GUARD: Ah, no thanks, Mr. Looney, haven't you done enough for us?

SERGEANT: Ah, sure, Mister Looney, sir, it'd be too much trouble going down for it.

LOONEY: Who said anything about going down for it? Don't I carry me little consolation prize with me? Bottle in this pocket, glasses in this. . . . (*Sounds of glass chinking.*)

SERGEANT: Well, Glory be to God.

GUARD: Mr. Looney, you're a magician.

LOONEY: I'm telling you, the Looneys is no fools. Here . . . (*Handing glasses round*) get that down yous.

SERGEANT: *Slawncha.*

GUARD: *Slawncha gus sale.*

LOONEY: *Slawncha gus sale agut.* Health and wealth to you.

SERGEANT: Land without rent to you.

GUARD: The woman of your heart to you.

LOONEY: A child every year to you.

GUARD: Married or single.

SERGEANT: A stout heart.

LOONEY: A wet beak.

SERGEANT: A death in Ireland.

ALL: *Slawncha!*

They drink.

SERGEANT (*Smacking his lips*): A good sup, Mr. Looney.

GUARD: Mr. Looney, sir, the sergeant wouldn't mind me asking you.

SERGEANT: It's depending what you are going to ask Mr. Looney for.

GUARD (*Shyly*): I was going to ask him to sing us a little bit of a song.

LOONEY: Ah, sure me dear decent man, think of the Mashter and Mishtress and the hour of the night it is.

GUARD: Ah, sure, with respects to them, they're that hard of sleeping they hardly heard the landmine. Sure a bitteen of a song won't wake them so easy.

LOONEY: Yes, but the time it is.

SERGEANT (*Bold from the whiskey*): Yerra, 'tis early before twelve and early after twelve.

LOONEY: All right, so boys, sure a bit of a song would cheer us up anyway. (*Sings*)

There is another explosion and a burst of machine-gun fire and shouting.

FIRST SHOUT: God forgive them murderers!

SECOND SHOUT: I hates bad grammar (*Laughs more or less maniacally*).

Machine-gun fire.

MRS. BALDCOCK (*Moans in her sleep*): Oh, (*to the tune of 'Galway Bay'*) Oh, maybe some day, I'll go back again to Ealing. . . .

ANANIAS: What's that, dear?

MRS. BALDCOCK: I was asleep.

ANANIAS: I never heard of anyone singing in their sleep.

MRS. BALDCOCK: I shouldn't be surprised if I danced in my sleep before I get out of this horrible country.

ANANIAS: Good night, dear.

MRS. BALDCOCK: Good night, Ananias . . . tomorrow . . .

ANANIAS: Tomorrow in Jerusalem. . . .

MRS. BALDCOCK: In where, dear?

ANANIAS: In Holyhead, dear.

Tonesollock House. It is early morning and the birds are singing. They keep on tweeting for a little but not so noticeably.

LOONEY: Ah, good morning, sergeant, isn't that a lovely morning? Glory be to God. A pity the Mashter and Mishtress didn't delay a few weeks more before they thought of going away to Ealing.

SERGEANT: 'Tis so, then, Looney. Sure, if they had have waited a bit longer, only a few weeks, sure everything is back to normal. Sure we're having our first eviction since 1917 tomorrow.

LOONEY: D'you tell me that now, sergeant dear?

SERGEANT: I do, bedad. The first eviction in six years, and I'll be in charge of it.

LOONEY: Sure, it's just like ould times, sergeant dear.

SERGEANT: And the I.R.A. is bet, thank God. That De Valera fellow got out a proclamation yesterday. De Valera telling his gangs of rogues, rebels, robbers, and wreckers that they're bet, and calling them to give up. It's in the paper here . . . (*Reads*) . . . 'Soldiers of the Legion of the Rearguard, Bulwark of the Nation's Honour. . . .'

[97]

LOONEY: God help us all. Soldiers . . . honour . . . (*Spits*) . . . murderers and robbers would be more like it.

SERGEANT: What else would you call them? Lot of scum. But anyway, it means one thing; the trouble is over. That's the end of the Civil War.

LOONEY: A civil war, did you call it? Bedad, and if that's what you call a civil war, sergeant dear, I hope I never see an uncivil one.

ANGEL: Call that a war? I've seen worse rows in the canteen of a Saturday night over someone pinching a pint.

LOONEY: Did you so then, sir? It could be. I believe they manage things better across the other side. Sure God help the Irish, if it was raining soup, they'd be out with forks. But I didn't think you'd had a war over in England this long time.

ANGEL: No, we 'ad it in France mostly. We nearly always 'ave our wars in someone else's country.

SERGEANT: If it's no harm asking, now what might your business be around here?

ANGEL: It's every 'arm. I'm in a 'urry to do some business 'ere in Tonesollock 'ouse and I'm not doing with neither of you, so I'll be off. Ta, ta.

SERGEANT: What did he say 'Ta, ta' for? I didn't give him anything.

LOONEY: That's his English way of saying 'goodbye'.

SERGEANT (*Ponderously*): Taah, taah.

LOONEY: Angel is his name. At least that's what Mister Chuckles calls him.

SERGEANT: Angel, that's a peculiar class of a name, more especially for a fellow the like of that. That's a fellow wouldn't lose his way in a jail, I'm telling you.

LOONEY: Angel is the name of the place in London he comes from. He's a great buddy of Mister Chuckles.

SERGEANT: Since Mister and Missus Baldcock went away over to England, I've heard nothing but 'Mister Chuckles' here, and 'Mister Chuckles' there. Who the hell is this Mister Chuckles, if it's no harm asking?

LOONEY (*Lowers his voice*): Ah, sergeant dear, you may well ask. A Dublin jackeen be the name of Chuckles Genockey is all I know about him, from the tenement houses off of the North Circular Road.

SERGEANT: And what class of a man is that to leave to run an estate? What would the likes of him know about land or cattle?

[98]

LOONEY: 'Tis not what he knows about land at all, at all, sergeant dear, but he knows the world and all about cattle.

SERGEANT: And how could he know about cattle without knowing about land?

LOONEY: Ah, sergeant, 'tis not on the land but in the market the money's made. What poor farmer ever made a fortune and isn't it a common thing for buyers and blockers and every kind of trickster to maybe double their money at a fair without ever handling a beast only buying off a farmer cheap and selling to a foreign buyer dear?

SERGEANT: Indeed, 'tis true for you.

LOONEY: Till the women going into the butcher are paying for meat the way it would be as cheap for them to be eating gold.

SERGEANT: Musha, 'tis true for you Looney. I often saw my father selling a beast to a robber of a buyer. (*Starts*) God bless us, what am I saying? Them men can't be classed as robbers. They are respectable with sons in the priesthood and T.D.'s, aye, and landlord gentry like Mr. and Mrs. Baldcock. (*Reproachfully*) 'Tis a shame for you, Looney, to be leading me into the sin of criticizin' respectable men with motor-cars and money.

LOONEY: I didn't mean it, sergeant.

SERGEANT: Do you know there's royalty that deals in store cattle and bishops. It's sinful, Looney, for us to talk like that.

LOONEY: I'm very sorry, sergeant.

SERGEANT: Ah, sure, I know you didn't mean any harm. And sure the Looneys were always known to be decent respectable people that knew their place and served their masters while there was life in their bodies. I often heard Mister Baldcock here saying: 'A Looney', says he, 'a Looney would work till he'd drop!'

LOONEY: It was only that I was trying to explain to you, sergeant, how the likes of Mr. Chuckles Genockey came to be agent here. He was always running round the cattle market from the time he was able to walk, and from doing messages for cattlemen, he rose up to be a class of a spy or a go-between from one buyer to another, and he used to do Mister Baldcock's business for him in the market; and now he's taken over Tonesollock House and the estate as well. It's a bit queer to see a man from the slums of Dublin that never had as much land as would fill a window-box, doing the lord and master over Tonesollock, but sure as you said, sergeant, it doesn't do to be criticizing our betters.

SERGEANT: Oh, I didn't mean a bowsy the like of that. Sure, that fellow is an impostherer of low degree. Only meant that it's not everyone that makes money is a robber. Most of them are not. The best rule is that them that had money previously are entitled to make more. Them that makes it for the first time are hill and dale robbers until they've had it for at least twenty years.

LOONEY: Well, you'd include Mister Chuckles with the hill and dale robbers.

SERGEANT: Injubettiddley. And that ruddy English Angel that came down to see him this morning.

LOONEY: He's a plumber. He came down to repair the roof. Look, the two of them is up there now.

On the roof. Seagulls screaming and roof noises generally.

ANGEL: . . . Now, this bit of flashing 'ere . . . there'll be nearly a 'alf ton of bluey in that alone.

CHUCKLES: And how much is lead at the moment?

ANGEL: 'Alf a quid a 'alf 'undred. That's about what we'll get. But they must 'ave 'ad a bleedin lead-mine of their own the way they poured it on this 'ere roof. I suppose we should get a thousand quid for the lot.

CHUCKLES: That should buy a few loaves anyway.

ANGEL: 'Course it will take a few days to get it all into the city, so I reckon on starting right now.

CHUCKLES: You get it ripped off and shag it down off the roof, and I'll get some of the farm labourers to load it on the lorry and we'll be in to Dublin with the first load, quick and speedy. I'll go below and collect them. . . .

ANGEL: Right . . . oh, I'll make a start anyway. (*Starts. Sounds of lead being ripped off roof.*) Uu . . . uup you come. Eas . . . eesy does it. Hey, Chuckles?

CHUCKLES: Hell . . . oooh?

ANGEL: Shall I start flinging it dahn nahw?

CHUCKLES: When I shout up, 'Throw it down', you can begin. (*To Looney*) Hey . . . you.

LOONEY: Is it me, Mashter Chuckles?

CHUCKLES: The very same. Tell that peeler there to get offside if he does not want a hundredweight of lead to come crashing down on his napper.

SERGEANT: Look at here, me good man. . . .

Looney: Stand away now, sergeant dear, for Mashter Chuckles.

Chuckles: (*Shouts*) Right away there, Angel, throw it dow . . . wn!
Lead crashes from roof to ground.

Sergeant: Look at here, Mister Looney, is it mending that roof or destroying it they are? Lifting the lead off it. Ripping and robbing maybe.

Chuckles: Hey, sleep-in-your skin.

Looney: Yes, Mashter Chuckles?

Chuckles: Go down and get some of them bullocks' nurses up here to get that lead on to the lorry.

Sergeant: Who did he say?

Looney: Bullocks' nurses he calls the cattle boys.

Sergeant (*Raising his voice to include Chuckles*): Before you go for anyone and before you put an ounce of lead up on that lorry, would it be any harm for me to be asking where it's going and where you're bring it to? (*Sarcastically*) That is, Mister Chuckles, if you don't mind.

Chuckles: I do mind . . . and you mind . . . mind your own bleedin' business.

Sergeant: Look at here, me good man, I'm responsible for the protection of property in the district of Tonesollock.

Chuckles: And I'm responsible for the property of Tonesollock House and the estate and lands thereof, and our solicitors are Canby, Canby, and Dunne, Molesworth Street, near the Freemasons' Hall, and if you interfere with me, I'll call them on the telephone and tell them you're persecuting the ex-Unionist minority, and get a question asked in the Senate. The Minister for Justice will love you for that.

Sergeant (*In suppressed wrath, but just a little anxious*): I'll attend to you in a minute, me man. (*To Looney*) What's this ex-Unionist minority? What does that mean, in plain English?

Looney: It means the gentry.

Sergeant: And is that Dublin guttersnipe . . . telling me . . . telling me . . . that I'm persecuting the gentry? Does he make out that he's one of them?

Looney: Well I suppose he means that he's running the estate for the master, and he's in the master's place like while the master is away.

Sergeant (*Sighs*): And God knows I was right. When I saw the dead lancers lying in O'Connell Street and heard the naval artillery

[101]

pounding the Post Office, I said to myself, something is going to happen, and when I heard the crash of the. . . .

Terrific noise as another load of lead crashes to ground.

SERGEANT (*Roars*): Hey, you, up there, hey! . . .

ANGEL: Hey you down there, want to get a 'undredweight of lead on your noggin?

SERGEANT: You just mind. . . .

CHUCKLES: You just get to hell out of here. You're on private land. If something falls on your cabbage head, you needn't come looking to us for compensation.

SERGEANT (*Indignant and despairing*): Look at here, Mister Looney, will you tell that impiddent bowsy who I am?

LOONEY (*in distress*): Oh, sergeant dear, it's not my fault and don't go bringing me into it. I don't want to lose me situation that I've been in this fifty years.

CHUCKLES: Hey you. Go-be-the-wall-and-tiddle-the-bricks.

LOONEY: Do you hear the way he calls me out of me name? The old respected name of Looney that was here before the Danes. How would I be trying to get that fellow to give respect to you when I can't get it for myself?

SERGEANT (*Sighs*): I'll be off for now, Mister Looney, but when Mister Baldcock comes back . . . I'll have a something or two to say to him.

LOONEY: Aye, when Mister Baldcock comes back. I'll be as dead as poor Black Joe waiting for him.

CHUCKLES: Hey, you Step-and-fetch it, do you not hear me calling?

LOONEY: Yes, Mister Chuckles, sir, I hear you calling me, sir, but what you call me, sir, is not my name.

CHUCKLES: Never you mind what I'm calling you.

LOONEY: I am a Looney, sir, and descended from a long line of Looneys, and I got a medal from the Royal Dublin Society at the Horse Show. . . .

CHUCKLES: What as . . . a prize goat?

LOONEY: For fifty years' service, sir, to the one family. The Baldcocks that own this estate.

CHUCKLES: I don't give a God's curse if you were here since Judas was in the Fire Brigade, and I won't give a damn if you're not here five minutes more. I'd be just as well pleased to be rid of you and a few more of them valleys and footmen up in the house, and maids and housekeepers . . . (*Thoughtfully*) . . . No, I'd keep the maids, except the old one.

LOONEY: The housekeeper you mean sir. Miss Gilltrap.

CHUCKLES: Yes, the one with a face like a plateful of mortal sins.

LOONEY: A most respected and superior class of woman, sir.

CHUCKLES: She looks it. But anyway, get some of them fellows up here and have that lead loaded on the lorry for us. Myself and the plumber have to be going into Dublin, directly.

LOONEY (*Resignedly*): I'll go and get them, sir. (*Moves off muttering to himself*) Curse a God on you, you low Dublin jackeen. You'd sack Miss Gilltrap, would you? But you'd keep the young maids, you would. (*Mutters and snuffles off. Lorry starts and moves off.*)

ANGEL: I thought they'd never get 'er bleedin' loaded. You know, it's a funny thing but the Irish over 'ere in Ireland, they ain't a bit like the Irish over at 'ome in England. Over 'ere they'd stand around all day, if they was let.

CHUCKLES: The fellows out on the farm and looking after the beasts are all right. They'll do a bit of a fiddle with me when we're taking cattle to the market. It's those butlers and valleys that I don't like.

ANGEL: Specially that old Looney. 'E gives me the creeps 'e does.

CHUCKLES: Ah well, I'll have the whole lot cleared out in another week.

ANGEL: I know business is business, Chuckles, and we'll have it off for a few thousand nicker each, but don't you feel like, well, old Baldcock trusted you a lot?

CHUCKLES: Of course, he trusted me a lot. How the hell could we've arranged the job at all if he didn't trust me? This is not like screwing some gaff along the Tottenham Court Road ... a rapid creep in, blow the peter and then scarper and read about it in the papers next morning. This is plundering a whole estate. Cattle, horse, sheep, pigs, even let the grazing. The furniture, pictures, the delph, glassware, all that I've had crated with old Baldcock's address in England stencilled on the sides so as they all think he's having it sent to him in England. Now there's the lead and tomorrow or the day after I'm bringing a geezer out to value the doors.

ANGEL: When he comes back, he'll come back to a ruin.

CHUCKLES: That's it.

ANGEL: I'm only asking mind, do you not feel in a way, it's a bit rough on them?

CHUCKLES: How is it? They got a picture of the old man that built the house. It's in books in the library and the Baldcocks boast about it that Cromwell's soldiers croaked about two villagefuls of people to get that land. And old Baldcock got the land off Cromwell's soldiers by using his loaf . . . the same as I'm using mine.

ANGEL: Well, you can 'ardly blame the old man for what happened years ago.

CHUCKLES: I'm not blaming anyone. I don't go in for this lark 'on our side was Erin and virtue, on their side the Saxon and guilt'. I just don't see why old Baldcock should have a lot of lolly and live in a big house while I go out to graft every morning and come home to a rat trap.

ANGEL: Well, you're a Communist, that's what you are.

CHUCKLES: I'm not a Communist. I'm too humble and modest. The Communists want to free all the workers of the world. I'm content to make a start and free one member of it at a time . . . myself.

ANGEL: You're just a tealeaf, then.

CHUCKLES: That's right, I'm a thief, same as you, and same as Mr. and Mrs. Baldcock. Only as they inherited their lolly, they are really receivers. And they say the receiver is worse than the thief. And now we're coming towards our own fence. Mister Eyes of Green, Marine Dealer.

ANGEL: What sort of a bleeding name is 'Eyes of Green'?

CHUCKLES: I don't know; it's just what everyone else calls him around the Liberty. I suppose they call him 'Eyes of Green' because he's an Irish Jew from Dublin City.

ANGEL: We never 'eard of Irish Jews in London.

CHUCKLES: Well you don't notice, I suppose. Most Dublin Jews have an accent like mine, only a bit worse.

Noise of lorry slowing up and stopping.

ANGEL: 'Ere 'e is, anyway. Mind if I see if 'e answers to his name? Hallo, Mister Eyes of Green.

EYES OF GREEN: Hello, you Black and Tan.

CHUCKLES: Listen, Eyes, nark the patriotism just now. We want to do a little business.

ANGEL: We've got a lot of bluey to sell you, Mister Eyes of Green, so don't be so leery.

EYES OF GREEN: All right I'll get it over here and weigh it.

Lorry backs over beside scales and lead is weighed.

ANGEL: That's the lot then.

EYES OF GREEN: Eighty quid, that's right?

ANGEL: No, it's not right.

CHUCKLES: Do you know, if you gave up being a Jew, you could be a jockey. You've a neck as hard as a jockey's rump.

EYES OF GREEN: What's the difference?

ANGEL: You're not even going by your own scales. And that's good lead.

EYES OF GREEN: Where did you get it and when are you going to give it back?

CHUCKLES: We got it from the estate I'm managing, and I'll show you the papers and give a proper receipt for the proper price.

EYES OF GREEN: I say eighty, what's the difference?

CHUCKLES: A score of pounds.

EYES OF GREEN: Split it. I'll give you ninety.

CHUCKLES: Done, and I hope the odd ten nicker chokes you.

EYES OF GREEN: That's real decent of you. (*Counts money*). Here you are. And many thanks for your Christian sentiments.

CHUCKLES: *Shalom alechim*, Eyes of Green.

EYES OF GREEN: *Slawn latt*, Chuckles.

CHUCKLES: Start her up, Angel, and we'll get over to the Northside for a drink.

Lorry starts again and off. Stops. Public house. Sounds of bottles, glasses. Hum of conversation: when Chuckles and Angel enter, there are shouts of welcome, male and female.

SHOUTS: Me hard man, Chuckles Genockey. Ah, Chuckles, is it yourself that's in it? Musha, me tight Chuckles. You're more nor welcome.

CHUCKLES: Shut up and give us a chance to order a drink for the people.

MALE SHOUT: Silence there for the decent man.

BARMAN: Yes, Chuckles, and what will it be?

CHUCKLES (*Looks round counting*): One, two, three, four. . . . It'd be cheaper to buy the pub. Well, make that . . . er . . . sixteen half ones of malt and chasers.

BARMAN: Certainly, Chuckles . . . (*Shouts*) sixteen small whiskeys and sixteen bottles of stout.

GRANNY GROWL: There you are, Mrs. Grunt, that's yours.

GRANNY GRUNT: Thank you, Mrs. Growl.

GRANNY GROWL: Don't thank me, thank Chuckles.

GRANNY GRUNT: Thank you, Mister Chuckles, sir, and *slawncha*.

GRANNY GROWL: *Slawncha*, Chuckles.

GRANNY GRUNT: *Slawncha*, Chuckles.

MALE AND FEMALE SHOUTS: *Slawncha*, Chuckles, the flower of the flock; the heart of the roll. *Slawncha*, and *slawncha*, again and again.

ANGEL: They don't 'alf like their wallop. Especially the old dears. Reminds me of 'ome. The Bricklayer's Arms or the Elephant of a Saturday night.

CHUCKLES: Wait till they get rightly oiled. (*Shouts*) Hey, more gargle for the people.

GRANNY GRUNT: Me life on you, Chuckles, and the divil thump and thank the begrudgers.

GRANNY GROWL: Up the Republic and to hell with the rest. Give us a rebel song, Mrs. Grunt, ma, a real Fenian one, the one you got the six months for. Up Stallion!

GRANNY GRUNT: I will, *alanna*, if you'll hand me that tumbler. (*She swallows a drink*) Thanks. (*Clears her throat: sings*).

GRANNY GRUNT AND CHORUS:

> When I was young I used to be
> > as fine a man as ever you'd see,
> And the Prince of Wales, he says to me
> > 'Come and join the British Army'. . . .
> Toora loora loora loo,
> They are looking for monkeys in the zoo.
> And if I had a face like you,
> > I'd join the British Army.
>
> Nora Condon baked the cake,
> > but 'twas all for poor Nell Slattery's sake
> I threw myself into the lake,
> > pretending I was barmy.
> Toora loora loora loo,
> 'Twas the only thing that I could do,
> To work me ticket home to you,
> > And lave the British Army.

Shouting, male and female, likewise screeches and roars.

SHOUT: Granny Grunt, your blood's worth bottling.

ROAR: Me life on you, Granny Grunt.

SCREECH: A noble call, now, you have, ma'm.

CHUCKLES: Granny Grunt, nominate your noble call.

GRANNY GRUNT: I call on the Granny Growl. Mrs. Growl, ma'am, Maria Concepta, if I call you be your first name.

GRANNY GROWL (*With dignity*): Certingly, Teresa Avila, to be sure.

CHUCKLES: Get something to lubricate your tonsils first. (*Shouts*) More gargle, there!

GRANNY GROWL: God bless you, me son.

GRANNY GRUNT: May the giving hand never falter.

FIRST VOICE: Up the Republic!

SECOND VOICE: Up Everton!

THIRD VOICE: Up the lot of yous. (*Drinks are handed round.*)

CHUCKLES: Did everyone get their gargle? (*Shouts of assent.*)

CHUCKLES: Well, Granny Growl, give us your song. Carry on with the coffin . . . the corpse'll walk.

GRANNY GROWL AND CHORUS (*Sings*):

> 'Oh Mrs. McGrath!' the sergeant said,
> 'Would you like to make a soldier out of your son Ted,
> With a scarlet coat and a big cocked hat,
> Now Mrs. McGrath, wouldn't you like that?'

> *With your too-ri-a-fol-de-diddle a,*
> *Too-ri-oo-ri-oor-ri-a*
> *With your too-ri-a, fol-de-diddle-a*
> *Too-ri-oo-ri-oo-ri-a.*

> So Mrs. McGrath lived on the sea-shore
> For the space of seven long years or more,
> Till she saw a big ship sailing into the bay;
> 'Here's my son Ted, wisha, clear the way.'

> 'Oh Captain dear, where have you been,
> Having you been sailing on the Mediterreen
> Or have ye any tidings of my son Ted,
> Is the poor boy living or is he dead?'

> Then up comes Ted without any legs
> And in their place he has two wooden pegs;
> She kissed him a dozen times or two
> Saying, 'Holy Moses 'tisn't you.'

> 'Oh then were ye drunk or were ye blind
> That you left yer two fine legs behind,
> Or was it walking upon the sea
> Wore yer two fine legs from the knees away?'

[107]

'Oh I wasn't drunk and I wasn't blind
But I left my two fine legs behind
For a cannon ball on the fifth of May
Took my two fine legs from the knees away.'

'Oh then Teddy me boy,' the widow cried,
'Yer two fine legs were yer mammy's pride
Them stumps of a tree wouldn't do at all
Why didn't ye run from the big cannon ball?'

'All foreign wars I do proclaim
Between Don John and the King of Spain
And by herrins I'll make them rue the time
That they swept the legs from a child of mine.

'Oh then, if I had you back again
I'd never let ye go to fight the King of Spain,
For I'd rather my Ted as he used to be
Than the King of France and his whole Navee.'

With your too-ri-a-fol-de-diddle a,
Too-ri-oo-ri-oor-ri-a
With your too-ri-a, fol-de-diddle-a
Too-ri-oo-ri-oo-ri-a.

GRANNY GROWL (*Sobs a bit*): Me tired husband, poor ould Paddins, he was shot in the Dardanelles.

GRANNY GRUNT (*Sympathetically*): And a most painful part of the body to be shot.

GRANNY GROWL: And me first husband was et be the Ashantees. All they found of him was a button and a bone.

GRANNY GRUNT: God's curse to the hungry bastards.

GRANNY GROWL: But still and all ma'm what business had he going near them? Me second husband had more sense. He stopped in the militia, and never went further than the Curragh for a fortnight.

GRANNY GRUNT: Maria Concepta, do you remember when he used to wait on them coming off of the train at Kingsbridge and they after getting their bounty money, and waiting in on the station to be dismissed.

GRANNY GROWL: 'Deed and I do, Teresa Avila, and me provoked sergeant, he was an Englishman, would let a roar that'd go through you.

ANGEL (*An N.C.O.'s roar*): 'Ri ... ght'? To yore respective work-houses, pore'ouses, and 'ore 'ouses ... d ... iss ... miss'!

GRANNY GRUNT: That's the very way he used to shout. It used to thrill me through me boozem.

GRANNY GROWL: Poor ould Paddins me tired husband. . . .

CHUCKLES: Granny Growl, never mind your husband for a minute. (*Raises his voice*) How would yous all like to come to a house cooling?

MALE AND FEMALE SHOUTS: We'd love to.

GRANNY GROWL: Teresa Avila, what's a house cooling?

GRANNY GRUNT: The opposite to a house warming I suppose. Like an American wake, when someone is going away. Chuckles is going away tonight. I heard them saying. But anyway there will be gargle on the job.

GRANNY GROWL: Oh begod, I'm game ... game for anything! (*She raises her voice to a shout*). . . . Game for anything. Bottle or draught.

CHUCKLES: All get settled in the lorry. All out to the lorry. The ladies gets in first and settles themselves and the men carries out the drink. Hey there, put up the gargle on the counter for the men to carry out to the lorry. Ten dozen of stout and ten bottles of whiskey.

Outside in the lorry.

GRANNY GRUNT: Are you right there, Maria Concepta?

GRANNY GROWL: I'm great, Teresa Avila. At our age we enjoy a good ride. It's that seldom we get one.

MALE VOICES: Take up that parcel. Here, mind the drink.

GRANNY GRUNT: Yous young women there at the end of the lorry, take the gargle off of the men.

Sounds of bottles rattling as they're put aboard the truck.

MALE VOICES: Everything stored aboard, Chuckles.

ANGEL (*From the cab*): Right, jump up behind and we're off. (*Lorry starts off into the night*).

BARMAN (*Shouts from the door*): Good night, good night.

MALE AND FEMALE SHOUTS: Good night, good night, good night and good luck. (*Lorry gathers speed*)

Tonesollock House. The lorry approaches, dimly heard in the night.

LOONEY (*From his window*): Here they are back. (*Chorus from the lorry, faint but growing slowly as the lorry comes nearer the house. . . . . . 'He was a quare one'. . . .*)

LOONEY: Another drunken lot of scum and old women amongst them. The dirty filthy lot. They'll be roaring and singing and cursing now till morning. Ah, Tonesollock House. . . .

In the house.

GRANNY GROWL: Ah me tired husband, he was in the Boer War, and he was standing there in the middle of South Africa, in a big long line, thousands upon thousands of them, every man like a ramrod, stiff as pokers, not a man to move even when a comrade fell, stretched on the parade ground, prostituted from the heat, and up rides Lord Roberts.

GRANNY GRUNT: A lovely man. I seen him in the Park and a pair of moustaches on his face a yard long. Waxed and stiff, they went through me boozem.

GRANNY GROWL: He rides along half the length of the line till he comes to my Paddins, and lets a roar out of him that would move your bowels: 'Fuslier Kinsella!' he roars.

GRANNY GRUNT: God bless us!

GRANNY GROWL: 'Fuslier Kinsella', he shouts. Paddins steps forward, smacks the butt of his rifle, and Lord Roberts looks down at him off his big white horse, and his moustache trembling with glory. 'Fuslier Kinsella', he roars, 'wipe your bayonet . . . you've killed enough!'

GRANNY GRUNT: My poor fellow, he was a ral, in the Fusiliers.

GRANNY GROWL: What's a ral, Teresa Avila?

GRANNY GRUNT: Well, it's either an admiral, a corporal or a general, but he was a ral, anyway. Passus that bottle there. Maria Concepta, and we'll have a sup between us anyway. (*They drink*) Where's Chuckles and that English chap be the way?

Upstairs.

CHUCKLES: I suppose we better get down now to the others. I suppose most of them is laid out, be this time. What time is it, Angel?

ANGEL: It's a quarter to five. The sun is coming up.

CHUCKLES: Well, I've everything here. The money from the cattle, from the sale of the farm equipment, and the house fittings, five thousand quid . . . two for you. . . .

ANGEL: That'll be a help. D'you know the last honest graft I was in was the railway . . . thirty-five bob a week.

CHUCKLES: And three for me. We better go down and say goodbye to them down below. (*They go downstairs.*)

GRANNY GRUNT: There you are, Chuckles.

CHUCKLES: We're off to the boat. We come down to bid yous goodbye.

GRANNY GROWL: Bedad and we'll give yous a send-off. Rouse up there the lot of yous.

MALE AND FEMALE SHOUTS: Wake up there! Wake up there! And sing!

GRANNY GROWL: Wake up Teresa Avila, wake up! Pass a bottle round there, till we wish Chuckles 'Good luck'.

MALE AND FEMALE SHOUTS: Good luck, Chuckles, *Slawncha*. Good luck, and God go with you.

GRANNY GRUNT AND CHORUS (*Sings*):

> Hand me down me petticoat, hand me down me shawl,
> Hand me down me petticoat, for I'm off to the Linen Hall.
> *With your he was a quare one, fol-de-do and g' ou' a that,*
> *He was a quare one, I tell you.*

Holyhead Station. Rattle, roar, etc., of trains. Wheesh of brakes.

PORTER: This way for the Dublin boat. This way for the mail boat. This way for the Dublin boat.

MRS. BALDCOCK: You've seen about the luggage, Ananias?

ANANIAS: Yes dear.

MRS. BALDCOCK: It will be nice to be home in dear old Ireland again.

ANANIAS: Yes, dear.

MRS. BALDCOCK: That horrid little house of Tabitha's, and Hereward so rude about your discharging your shotgun in the garden! And those awful, frightful, horrible children.

ANANIAS: Yes, dear, I knew you'd prefer to be back in Tonesollock.

MRS. BALDCOCK: It will be just like when first we wed, and you brought me there as a bride.

ANANIAS: Dear Boadicea.

MRS. BALDCOCK: Darling Ananey!

ANANIAS: Dearest, darlingest Boadey!

MRS. BALDCOCK: (*Greatly astonished*): Look, Ananias.

ANANIAS: Where, darling, at what, dear?

MRS. BALDCOCK: They're just coming out of the customs shed.

ANANIAS (*A trifle impatient*): Who's coming out of the customs shed, darling?

MRS. BALDCOCK: The agent . . . your man of affairs . . . at home . . .
at Tonesollock.

ANANIAS: Genockey, in England?

MRS. BALDCOCK: Wales, darling.

ANANIAS (*Impatiently*): Whatever it is. Leaving that customs shed!

MRS. BALDCOCK: There he is there, don't you see him with another
man, there, they're speaking to a porter.

ANANIAS: Why, bless my soul, so it is.

MRS. BALDCOCK. They're coming this way, dear, speak to him.

ANANIAS: Genockey, Genockey, I didn't hear you coming over.
You didn't write.

ANGEL (*Speaking politely*): I'm afraid you're making a mistake, sir.
My employer does not speak English.

ANANIAS: Does not speak English? Ridiculous. Genockey was born
and bred in the city of Dublin, where they speak the best English
after Oxford.

ANGEL: I'm afraid you are mistaken, sir. This is Doctor Hohnhohn,
(*He makes for 'Hohnhohn', a sound indistinct but very French*) Professor
of Celtic Studies at the Sorbonne . . . Belfast Celtic and Glasgow
Celtic.

ANANIAS: I beg your pardon, sir.

ANGEL (*To Chuckles*): *Vous êtes le professeur Hohnhohn, oui?*

CHUCKLES: *Oui, je suis.*

ANGEL (*Speaking in his normal Cockney accent*): See, he says so 'imself.
We got to catch this train for London. . . . Ta, lady, ta gov.

Train moves off. Gathers speed. Fades.

The Big House.

THE BIG HOUSE: Through war, riot and civil commotion have I
stood, and have lived through bad times to see these good times. To
get rid of common people and their noisy children and have back
again, safe from the towns and cities, my dear horse-faced ladies,
and my owners. Stout, redfaced men, and the next best thing to
animals, and best of all, the land, for the horse, sheep and bullock,
which my people even come to resemble in the end . . . my beeves, oh
my beeves, my sheep, my horses, and oh my bullocks, my bullocks,
my bullocks. . . .

Tommy Kane, birdcatcher

Galway: by the Spanish Arch

3

The Bleak West

GALWAY CITY – it's really a town – is a hard place to explain, but if I tell you that I was once sold sixty acres of land there at a fair in the town itself, you'll probably begin to have some idea that it is an unusual place. Nowadays, it's a haunt of commercial travellers relaxing at week-ends, a few Aran Islanders over to sign some stupid forms, and farmers who come in there to buy potatoes from Michael Joe Burke who was wounded in some boating accident in the Mediterranean during the war. Michael insists that he doesn't remember it, that he was too drunk – he was in the British Navy and he has a pension; they don't apparently care about people being drunk in the Navy which is uncommon civil of them and to their lasting credit.

One of my best friends always was the late Monsignor Pádraig de Brún, who was President of University College, Galway until he retired and became Chairman of the Irish Arts Council until his death a couple of years ago. A man of great learning and, what is more important, charity, he was a mathematician who translated the whole of Dante's *Divine Comedy* into Irish as well as many ancient Greek plays. His brother is the Master-General of the Dominican Order and was the confessor of the late Pope Pius XII, and now has been made Cardinal.

The people of Galway are very proud of being from Galway though, personally, I think that it is silly enough being proud of being from anywhere in particular. You get all sorts from everywhere, as the Old Etonian said to the Wykehamist, both being con-men. But proud and all as the Galwegians are, there are pubs where they won't be admitted. I know one where they are hardly admitted at all because they're not respectable enough – I suppose in dress (they don't go in very much for the black tie and that) while there's another pub where they're not admitted for more puritanical reasons – the proprietor thinks they shouldn't be drinking. The centre of social life in Galway, however, is a pub called 'The Old Malt House' where everybody goes about nine o'clock of an evening. It's a warm-hearted place owned by Ned Walsh whose father was murdered in 1920 by the Black and Tans – they were the British Mau Mau of the time (oaths, mutilations and all, they had).

One of the first things you see coming into Galway is the statue erected in Eyre Square in memory of the late Pádraic Ó Conaire. He was a great Irish writer whose short stories are still among the best available in the Irish language. At one time he was a member of the British Civil Service but gave that up to go on the road with a donkey and cart which he thought was a better living. They say that he went to Russia and spoke to Tolstoy about the craft of writing and from what I know of him, I wouldn't put it past him at all. The poet F. R. Higgins, who was the manager of the Abbey Theatre until his early death in 1941, was a close friend of Pádraic's and wrote a great elegy on him, some of which is:

> They'll miss his heavy stick and stride in Wicklow –
> His story-talking down Winetavern Street,
> Where old men sitting in the wizen daylight
> Have kept an edge upon his gentle wit;
> While women in the grassy streets of Galway,
> Who hearken for his passing – but in vain,
> Shall hardly tell his step as shadows vanish
> Through archways of forgotten Spain.
>
> Ah, they'll say: Pádraic's gone again exploring;
> But now down glens of brightness, O he'll find
> An alehouse overflowing with wise Gaelic
> That's braced in vigour by the bardic mind,
> And there his thoughts shall find his own forefathers –
> In minds to whom our heights of race belong,
> In crafty men, who ribbed a ship or turned
> The secret joinery of song. . . .

One of Pádraic's stories that I remember concerned his days in the Civil Service and in it he describes how a colleague began to wear a kilt. Well, that might look all right in, say, Blackheath on a Saturday afternoon, but a trifle odd on Monday morning on the way to the City.

The Spanish Tavern

Pádraic met the wife one day and it appeared she said: 'My husband was all right until he discovered he was a bleeding Irishman.'

The statue in Eyre Square shows Pádraic with his hand stretched out as if he was making a point to his audience and it is the custom, on certain nights, for the local wags to put a bottle of stout – empty of course – in it from time to time; it seems to give them great amusement. On another occasion, during the middle thirties, the Blue Shirts, a Fascist organization in Ireland financed largely by the big British industrialists there, put a blue shirt over the statue. And talking of Fascists, not many people know that Galway was mentioned during the course of the Nuremberg trials after the war. The prosecuting counsel there mentioned that when William Joyce, Lord Haw-Haw, was trying to join the British military forces or something like that, he said; 'I gave great service to the British Army when I was in Galway against the Irish insurgents in 1920 and 1921' – which only goes to show that you can't keep a man out of the S.S. if that's what he's made for. I think Joyce's father was a member of the Royal Irish Constabulary at the time but, at all events, the whole family had to leave in a hurry and their house was burnt down.

Joyce was about as Irish as the late Senator Joe McCarthy. It's sickening how there are always people willing to attack others all the time, instead of minding their own business and rearing their families. There are Jews who wish to attack Arabs, just as formerly there were Germans who wished to attack Jews. There are Irish people who wish to attack English people, just as there are English people who wish to attack everyone. There are Germans who wish to attack twice as much everyone and I'm not sure that the best thing for the safety of, at least, Europe wouldn't be for Germany to return to the *status quo* as it was before 1870 and let them all attack one another. Or the Arctic – or better still the Antarctic – could be officially declared the World's Battleground and any war not taking place there, could immediately be proclaimed illegal! I offer that suggestion for free to President Kennedy and he might even be able to use it domestically, apart from a foreign policy plank, for I'm told that in the southern states of America there are people who like no one – they don't like blacks, they don't like Roman Catholics, they don't like Jews, they don't like themselves, if you can believe Tennessee Williams, and it's very difficult to make out whom they do like. One American I know that likes everybody, and that everybody ought to like, is Paul Robeson. He sings all the time about how men should love each other and he sings about the cruel things of this world – Spanish songs of revolt – and I've heard him singing that Irish song *Kevin Barry* that Carl Sandburg said had almost become the anthem of the lumpenproletariat of Chicago:

> In Mountjoy Jail, one Monday morning,
> High upon the gallows tree,
> Kevin Barry gave his young life
> For the cause of liberty.
> Only a lad of eighteen summers
> Yet no one can deny
> As he walked to death that morning,
> He proudly held his head on high. . . .

The peace anywhere along the shores of Galway Bay is something that would make you wish that all this cruelty would stop. There's no more wonderful feeling than swimming there out in the Atlantic Ocean – in a good year it's far better than Cannes or anywhere else on the Mediterranean. At Cannes or one of those places, you're surrounded by millions of people, the beaches are leased out and you can't even be sure of getting a place where you can take off your clothes in private. Not that I'm against people taking off their clothes before each other but, as you can see at Cannes, it becomes less attractive after the age of thirty. I don't like this at all and there should be something done about it – maybe the United Nations could pass a resolution against it. There are two things on which the Americans and the Russians might well join forces – first, to make people know as much at eighteen as they do at thirty-eight; and second, to make people as attractive-looking at thirty-eight or forty-eight as they were at eighteen – but I suppose the brewers would be against it. All else, though, is waste and nobody should be impressed by the Sputnik or the Bluenik or any other nick.

I often think of things like that lying on the flat of my back on the rocks at Carraroe. It's a tourist place, Irish-speaking – the tourists are good for the locality from the money point of view but not very good for the people, really. It's a place to be, though, – you can eat fresh lobster for every meal with lovely griddle-bread and porter. The only thing to avoid there is the boys that have recently arrived back from England – they're inclined to be full of Edgware Road English – they're not very co-operative, you might say.

An old friend of mine that lives there is Patrick Griffin. He's a man now about ninety, if he's still alive when this book appears. His wife

The Atlantic coast near
Bealadangan, Connemara

Máire doesn't speak any English but she has the sweetest Irish I ever heard. Patrick, long ago, was reputed to be the best potheen maker in the district. I remember talking to a son of his, who came home from America where he had been drafted into the Army, and I asked him what it was like.

'It was very good,' he said, 'and I found the Irish a great help to me.'

'How was that,' I said, 'in the American Army?'

'Because,' he said, 'a lot of the recruits are from south Boston and a great number from Connemara and from the Aran Islands and,' he said, 'we could speak Irish among ourselves and the N.C.O.s and officers didn't know what we were saying.'

I remember, too, meeting in Patrick Griffin's house an old lady who told me that she had been twenty years in America and she came back with hardly a word of English. Beside Patrick's house live the kindly O'Nuallain family. Many's the good swim I had with Diarmuid, the eldest son. He has recently been ordained and is now away with the missions in Nigeria.

Patrick's house stands on a little bay and the Atlantic comes in right beside it. In a graveyard just at the back is buried the author, Maurice O'Sullivan, whose book *Twenty Years A-Growing* is published in Penguins and in the World's Classics series by the Oxford University Press.

Another good friend of mine in Carraroe is Stiofán O Fláithbheartaigh. He said to me after I came back from America, '*Cead fáilte sa bhaile romhat, A Bhreandáin:* a hundred welcomes home to you, Brendan!'

'*Cead* mile *fáilte,*' I said, 'surely, Stiofán: a hundred *thousand* welcomes!'

'*Muise,* isn't a hundred welcomes enough for any man?' said Stiofán.

A lot of well-known people beside myself go to Carraroe in the summer. Up to some years ago, a regular visitor was Freddie Boland, Ireland's Representative at the United Nations, who was President of that show last year. I think he's the only diplomat I've ever been photographed with, for when he was Ambassador in London, he came to the first night of *The Quare Fellow* and himself, my wife and myself, were all snapped talking together in the foyer. Siobhán MacKenna, her husband, Denis O'Dea and her son are in Carraroe frequently – Siobhán, of course, grew up in Galway and started her acting career there in the Gaelic Theatre. In fact, you can say nearly anybody that's anyway prominent in Irish life finds his way to Carraroe at some time.

Except for the money that the visitors leave behind them, the whole

Gathering sea-weed for manure near Carraroe

of the Galway sea-board is a poor enough place. With the young people leaving for Kilburn and Clapham, the number of Irish-speakers is going down. The only way in which the native language could possibly be preserved there is by some form of economic socialism, but the Government are willing to do anything in their power to save the language, except adopt the radical solution of organizing a state fishing industry along the coast. If it's economic for trawlers to come from France and Spain to fish off Galway, it ought to be possible for the Government at home to take the fishing industry out of the hands of private enterprise, organize it on a nationalized basis and send the fishermen out into the Atlantic – but their conservatism is stronger than their Gaelicism.

The people themselves catch fish, of course, but mostly on a very small scale for they haven't the proper equipment. It's in the interests of the big fishing firms in Dublin to keep things as they are – they prefer to sell a few fish dear than a lot of fish cheap. A couple of years ago, Peadar O'Donnell was trying to negotiate with East Germany for the sale of salted herrings, and some members of the Dail who are living quite comfortably themselves said that the curse of God would fall upon any dealings with the Communists. But these people who were so free with their admonitions were all living in Dublin suburban villas, and they weren't out at the crack of dawn digging up little patches of land. For with the few fish they catch, the people of Connemara cultivate infinitesimal patches of ground – they break up the rocks and gather sea-weed to try and fertilize the miserable clay to get a few potatoes and vegetables.

And the women have to work hard, too – usually they try to raise a few turkeys for which they get about a shilling a pound from the Dublin dealers, who then sell them for about four to five shillings. But with the expansion of the battery-fed turkey industry, I'm glad to say that the Dublin dealers' profits won't be so high. But I think that the women in the West will still be able to get about the same amount of money for their turkeys.

Let nobody tell you otherwise – the industry of the people of Connemara (and the poor people in the other parts of the country as well) is marvellous. They work very hard for the little bit of money they manage to scrape together and it's a great pity they're not helped more. But in other ways they're comfortable enough and I give the Government credit for that – the idea that Connemara is a rocky wilderness dotted with broken-down cabins in which the people exist,

Patrick Griffin

is all nonsense. There are no cabins in Connemara. Housing all over rural Ireland is extremely good. The people live in slated, electric, four-and-five-roomed houses, with running water and good sanitation and the Government provided those houses over the last thirty years.

Nevertheless, though I like the old Gaelic civilization as it was, I wouldn't be averse to seeing a few large chimney stacks around Connemara. One industry was introduced by the Government some years ago – the growing of tomatoes in greenhouses. The tomatoes are, maybe, a bit more expensive than the Dutch ones, but they have a finer flavour and, as production increases, they will grow cheaper – or they ought to.

One piece of advice I give freely to anyone visiting the West, is to keep away from potheen. No matter what anyone tells you about the fine old drop of 'Mountain Dew', it stands to common sense that a few old men, sitting up in the back of a haggard in the mountains with milk-churns and all sorts of improvised utensils, cannot hope to make good spirits, when most modern distilleries, equipped with every device that science can provide, can't find it easy to produce decent whiskey. Potheen is just murder – it's the end and you can take it from me, for I have a wide enough experience of it.

I once knew an old man who drank potheen at the rate of about a couple of pints a day for a fortnight, when he finally wasn't able to drink any more and he got so ill that he was on his back for another fortnight before he recovered.

I asked him, 'Why,' I said, 'if it makes you so sick, do you continue to drink it? Do you not remember the terrible hangovers you had?'

'Well, no,' he said, 'because to tell you the truth, when I've been off it for about a fortnight, I feel so good that I just have to go out and celebrate.'

One of the hazards of travelling in the west of Ireland is the danger of meeting a certain type of Irish-American – 'Returned Yanks' they call them. They're always offering advice in a very patronizing way and although some of them, the poor devils, have been chasing trains on the Boston underground or working for the New York sewerage during their four or five years in America, they have saved up for this great visit to show the people at home how much they know and how dynamic they now are. I was sitting in a hotel at Ballinasloe at breakfast one morning, not feeling very well at all, and waiting on the waitress to bring me some whiskey before I could even encourage myself to look at a bacon and egg. Seated at a table not far from me was a person very like the unlamented Senator Joe McCarthy, wearing a suit of fine American cloth and a huge green tie, and though he looked across at me several times, I didn't encourage him to speak. Normally, I'm quite anxious, or at least, willing to speak to strangers, but I wasn't able for this man at that hour of the morning.

Finally, he looked across and he said, 'Say'.

I said, 'Yes?'.

He said, 'You know you could do a lot for this country – you could do a lot with this country.'

'Well,' I said, 'you could blow it up,' – that remark being more the humour of the moment than my permanent attitude.

'Oh!' he said, 'you're one of these people that don't believe in Ireland's future. Why don't you people try to do something practical? You could clean up that river at the end of the town and you could get some good fishing there and a lot of Americans would come for that. . . .'

'Friend,' I said, 'I only came in on the six o'clock last night. Please give me a little time.'

I remember being with a great crowd of Republicans once down there in the West – we had been on some job or other. We were all devoted to the Cause, and after our business was finished, we adjourned for a few jars. For one reason or another, we sat up too long and it must have been nearly six o'clock when the proprietor put us all up to bed. Down the next morning we staggered, and I remember Tommy, one of the group, coming in looking as desperate as anyone I've ever seen after a night. He managed to sit down beside me at the table and the waitress came over and said: 'What would you like – bacon and egg?'

A shudder of nausea ran through Tommy's body and he put his face in his hands and practically sobbed out: 'Oh! Mary, Oh! Mary, my dear . . . I couldn't even look at the flag.'

People you'll meet a good deal of on the roads in the West are the tinkers. In many places, these people are romanticized, in others they're persecuted – in Northern Ireland, for instance, they're forbidden to exist at all. They are not, of course, in any way connected with the Romanies, but like them, they're poor travelling people. They are said to cause a lot of damage and to use piebald horses because they can let out a piebald in a farmer's field at night and, because they can see him better than a black or brown horse, can catch him easier in the morning. Oddly enough, I never yet met a tinker that could speak Irish, though they speak a very peculiar form of English. They used to be very good tinsmiths but nowadays they mostly deal in horses.

They're harmless enough, on the whole. Maybe they are a bit of a nuisance, but then everybody is a bit of a nuisance now and again (look at the county councillors), so that doesn't have to be held against them.

I was on the Aran Islands once when some tinkers that were actually tinsmiths came over. They were making cans and selling them and I said to an old man who wanted to buy a can: 'Will I talk to the tinker for you?'

'No, Brendan,' he said, 'I will English the man mineself.'

So he went down to the tinker and the tinker said: 'Do you want a can?'

The old Islander pointed to the tinker's roll of tin and said: 'Tinker, I see you have plenty leather.'

The tinker again asked him did he want a milk can? and held one out for inspection.

'No,' said the Islander, 'I do not want that one. It's too big. I want a young one.'

I stayed with tinkers myself a few nights when I was on the run in 1941 and 1942. They were very good at cooking rabbits which they snared, but they wouldn't eat fish under any circumstances. In fact, I think they'd die before they'd eat a bite of fish, probably having some sound instinct that the fish would go off in the conditions under which they'd have to keep it.

My father had experience of tinkers that came up to Dublin one time – and a very personal experience it was. His father had rented a whole Georgian house on the north side of Dublin and my grandmother, who was used to living in tenements all her life, couldn't understand how one family could want more than two rooms. She thought it was a great waste having the whole house and was always trying to get him to take in tenants, which he wouldn't agree to do. One time, however, the grandad went down the country to do a painting job on a church, and my grandmother was looking wistfully at two fine rooms upstairs that were vacant, and the next thing is that Mrs. MacGowan, a Queen Tinker, came up to the door, knocked on it, and tempted my grandmother with a free fortune, telling her she was to marry for the third time, and offering her a Paisley shawl for £5 in return for accommodation for herself and her entourage.

My grandmother was sorely tempted by the five pounds, and the next thing was, she took it, and Mrs. MacGowan said that she'd be around to the establishment some time later. So my grandmother gave her a key and left it at that.

Tinkers near Maam Cross

Later, about one in the morning, my father, who was sleeping in the house, was woken up by a terrible commotion on the stairs and he didn't know what was happening. At first, he thought the house was being kicked down by poltergeists, or demons, or devils, or something. There was a terrible racket in the hall and he went out and there, begod, if the MacGowans weren't bringing a gennet up the stairs. So a row started between them, but there were about six of the MacGowans, and only one of my father and one of my grandmother, and they said my grandmother had accepted their £5 for all that Mrs. MacGowan wanted to bring with her, and Mrs. MacGowan said they weren't going to leave the poor gennet out on the street all night, and my grandmother, or my father for that matter, needn't think it.

Well, they compromised by agreeing to leave the gennet in the hall, where they tied him to a handrail on one side and to a hatrack on the other, and left him facing the door.

The next morning, my father came down and found my grandfather, who had come back unexpectedly from the country, leaning against the hall door, which was open, and pointing in front of him in horror. And he said to my father: 'Stephen,' he said, 'tell me, I think I'm in the horrors. Could that possibly be a gennet?'

'Yes, it is,' said my father.

'Thank God,' said my grandfather, 'I thought I was in delirium tremors and I was seeing gennets instead of rats.'

Later on, my father had some words with the MacGowans about the gennet, and you could say they were in basic English, seeing that the MacGowans didn't understand Irish, the poor tinkers that they were.

Of all the places in the West, perhaps, the Aran Islands are my favourite. I've spent a good deal of time there and will again. These are three islands off the coast of Galway. The natives themselves insist that they are natives of Galway, and they follow the fortunes of the Galway hurling and football teams, and when those teams are playing in Dublin and a commentary on the match being broadcast, you'll find the older people who do not speak English, and the younger people who have not much English, getting the commentary translated by learned people who know the foreign tongue.

According to Liam O'Flaherty, author of *The Informer* and other books, who is a native of the Aran Islands himself, the male ancestors of most of the people there from 1600 onwards were English. They were part of Cromwell's army. Cromwell decided to leave the more revolutionary part of his army behind him, so he dumped them on the

In the drawing, a sign reads: IS FEARRDE TÚ Guinness

Aran islander

Aran Islands and gave them a bit of land each there, when he promptly sailed off to England and forgot all about them. To this day, there are Piggotts and Perkins there on the islands, and Liam O'Flaherty insists that even now they speak Irish with a Cockney accent. One thing I can say from my own experience is that I have noticed the number of fair-haired people on the islands compared with the mainland.

A film was made about the Aran Islands once, but I think it did more damage than anything else. It was *Man of Aran* and it was made by Robert Flaherty, a very great director indeed, who was very kind to the islanders while he was making the film. But the fact that he was making the film at all, sort of filled their heads up with notions that they were never going to see a poor day again, and that they would always have soft money. He brought some of them over to London for the showing of the film and, all in all, destroyed many a happy home in the end. You can't make a film about the Aran Islands every day of the week, but that wasn't explained to the islanders at all.

In the film, the islanders chase a basking shark to capture it for its oil. You could say that this was falsification, for basking sharks hadn't been chased around the islands for over sixty years and Flaherty had to bring in someone from Alaska, or thereabouts, to teach them the technique again. This would have been all right if Flaherty had not let the film turn the islanders' heads with dreams of fame and money. I knew one old woman on the islands and I remember her remarking to me one day – Maggie Dirrane, it was, who was in *Man of Aran* – 'Ah, Brendan, you're going home now and there'll be only one film star left on the island now,' – meaning herself.

It was on Aran that I chanced to hear how Lough Neagh and the Isle of Man came to be there at all. It seems that Finn MacCool, the great Irish giant who was about 20 feet tall, was challenged one time by the Scots giant, who was 40 feet tall. Finn accepted the challenge but said to his wife, 'Don't worry about it – he won't come over.' But the Scots giant did come and Finn's wife hurried into the house and 'Quick, Finn,' she said, 'here's the Scots giant.'

'Oh,' said Finn, 'what will I do?'

'I know what you'll do,' said his wife, 'jump into the child's cot'. So Finn put the child out of the cot and jumped in himself and his wife put a sucking bottle in his mouth.

So the Scots giant came in and he roared: 'Is Finn MacCool here?'

'No,' said Finn's wife, 'there's nobody here but myself and the baby,' pointing to Finn in the cot.

Kilronan, Aran

'Jesus,' said the Scots giant, 'if that's the child, what must the father be like,' and off he ran. Finn got out of the cot then and tore out a sod of grass and threw it after the Scots giant, and the hole that he pulled the sod from, filled up with rain and it became Lough Neagh, and the sod of grass fell into the sea between England and Ireland and became the Isle of Man.

On the big island, I was once in company with two fishermen, since dead, and one night we imprisoned the island's police force, which consisted of two guards, in their own cells and threw the keys down the cliffs. We didn't do this without some provocation, because they had come in to arrest us for singing a song in the village street.

It's a strange commentary on civilization that on the other two islands there are no police and I have never seen a row on either of them. On the big island, where there are police, the mainland licensing laws are enforced with a few additions, depending on the whims of the sergeant, and there are rows and police court cases every so often. On the other islands, the pubs open to suit the needs of the inhabitants, which means that, in the months of September and October, when they are picking the potatoes and work with the light, the pubs don't open until eleven o'clock at night and they shut about one or two in the morning. I have never heard a cross word in either of the pubs, nor any disturbance; and I've never seen anyone drunk except a stranger, a 'foreigner'.

The pub on the middle island is owned by a man known as 'Seamus a' Vayrla', which means, Seamus of the English language. Seamus had a son, a priest of whom he was very proud, and he had a notice in Latin about his son's ordination and he asked me if I could read it. I said that I could and that I could translate it into English and into Irish. I recognized only one word, Nigeria, so I said, both in English and Irish, 'This is to certify that Seamus a' Vayrla's son, young James, has been granted authority by the Pope to convert all and sundry in and about the district, townland and nation of Nigeria. Yours sincerely, Pope Pius XII.'

On the western island, Inishere, there was an old man I knew, Michael Meagher. He is dead now, but you'll come across mention of him in Synge – he tried to teach Synge Irish, a task which he found impossible, he told me. Michael was called on once to come to Dublin to some festival of Gaelic culture, to deliver a sermon or oration on temperance. He put on his best suit and he was very nervous for he had never been to Dublin before.

'How did you get through your speech on temperance?' I remember asking him when he told me about it.

Inishmore, Aran

'Well,' he said, 'I brought a half a bottle of potheen with me and before I got up on the stage to speak, I went into the lavatory and had a good slug of it and it gave me courage to go on.'

The Aran Islanders found Synge patronizing, which I can't say I find in his work. But they are very touchy and no matter what is said about them in any part of the world, they find out about it. For instance, they will certainly know everything I've said about them here, but it's said with love and respect and I hope it won't come between us.

On Inishere, there is a great storyteller called Joe. Joe would sit by the fire and start telling story after story and if interrupted, would have to start all over again. One good one – these stories have been handed down for generations – is about the King of Ireland's son and I'll tell it to you now.

Once upon a time, and a very good time it was too, when the streets were paved with penny loaves and houses were whitewashed with buttermilk and the pigs ran round with knives and forks in their snouts shouting: 'Eat me, eat me!' there lived a King of Ireland and he had three sons named Art, Neart and Ceart. Art is a man's name simply, Neart means strength and Ceart means right or justice. Well, Art was his father's favourite and the other two boys were very jealous of him. At one particular time, you could hear, all around the country, heavenly music coming from somewhere, and the King wanted to know where it was coming from. So he said to his three sons, 'Go out and whichever of you finds out where the heavenly music is coming from, can have half my kingdom.'

So the three of them set off out until they came to a big hole and from this big hole they could hear the sound of the music coming. Neart and Ceart said to Art: 'Will you go down? You're the lightest and the youngest and we'll let you down into this hole on a rope. You can see where the music is coming from and then we'll pull you up again,' hoping never to see him again.

Art said: 'Certainly, I will. I think that's a good idea.'

Down on the end of a rope he was lowered and he went along a cave like a long tunnel, along and along and along until it got very dark. He walked for hours until it must have been night-time, for in the tunnel he couldn't tell night from day. In the end and when his feet were falling off him, he saw a light. Over to the light he went and he met an old man and he said to the old man that was there: 'Could you tell me where the heavenly music is coming from?'

'No, then,' said the old man, 'I can't. But I tell you what you can do.

You can stop the night and tomorrow you can walk – it's a day's journey – on to my father's place and he might be able to tell you.'

So the old man put him up for the night and gave him the best of food. They had rashers and eggs with black pudding and white pudding and a Cork drisheen, three Hafner's sausages each, the best of homemade wholemeal bread, all washed down with lashings of strong tea, and after that they both went to bed, as well they might after such a feed.

The next morning Art woke up and started on his journey for another day's travelling along the tunnel, until he came to another light and he went in and met an old, old man and he said to him: 'Are you the father of the other old man that I saw back along there?'

'That's not an old man,' said the second old man, 'he's only a hundred.'

'Well', said Art, 'I'd like to know where the heavenly music is coming from and he said you might be able to help me.'

'Well,' said the second old man, 'that I can't help you. But my father that lives further up might be able to. Come in anyway and I'll feed you for the night and you can get up in the morning and go up and ask my father.'

So Art went in and the old, old man gave him a great meal. They had bowls of stirabout, followed by huge plates of the best Limerick Ham with spring cabbage and lovely potatoes, that were like balls of flour melting in your mouth and, with all this they drank three pints each of the freshest buttermilk Art had ever tasted. I can tell you he slept soundly that night.

And the next morning he got up and after saying goodbye to the old, old man, he walked for another whole day along the tunnel until he came to another light and there was an old, old, old man. So Art said to him: 'Are you the father of the old, old man back there along the tunnel?'

'Well, I am,' said the old, old, old man, 'but that fellow's not as old as he makes out; he's only a hundred and fifty and he eats all them new-fangled foods, as you probably found out.'

'Well,' said Art, 'he did me very well. But what I wanted to know was if you can tell me where the heavenly music comes from?'

'Well, now,' said the old, old, old man, 'we'll talk about that in the morning. Come on in now and have a bit to eat and rest yourself. You must be famished after that day's walking.'

So in Art went and the old, old, old man got some food ready. They started off with two great bowls of yellow buck* porridge each and after that, they had four crubeens† apiece with fresh soda bread and homemade butter and they had three pints of the creamiest porter Art had ever drunk to go with it all.

The next morning, he got up and he said to the old man: 'Now can you tell me where the heavenly music is coming from?'

'Well, no,' said the old, old, old man, 'but I know that there's nobody else living at the end of this tunnel except a terrible fierce man, a giant, and,' he said, 'I wouldn't go near him if I were you. But if you do decide to go up to him, he lives a terrible far distance away at the very end. You'll find, however,' he said, 'a little stallion when you go a couple of miles up the road there and, if you get up on him, he'll carry you to where the heavenly music comes from. But,' he said, 'you'll want to be very wary of that giant.'

Art went along and he came up to where, sure enough, there was a stallion and there was light with more light further on. So the stallion said to him: 'Do you want a lift?'

'I do,' said Art, 'but I'm going up to where the heavenly music is.'

'Well, that's all right,' said the stallion, 'no offence given and no offence taken. Jump up there on me back and I'll take you.'

So up on the stallion's back he jumped and the stallion galloped away for nearly a whole day, until he came to one of the most beautiful gardens Art had ever seen. 'This,' said the stallion, 'is the nearest I can take you to where the heavenly music comes from.'

Art went up through the garden, wondering at every more marvellous thing that he saw. Nearer and nearer came the heavenly music and at last Art came to a house and the music was coming from there. Into the house Art went and there was the most beautiful girl he had ever seen. And she was singing and making the heavenly music.

'Good morning,' said Art and then he said quickly, 'don't let me interrupt your song which is the loveliest I've ever heard.'

'Oh!' she answered him, 'I'm glad you've interrupted it. I have to make music here for an old giant that captured me. I'm the King of Greece's daughter,' she said, 'and I've been here for a year and a day and I can't get away from this old fellow until someone comes to rescue me. But,' she said, 'I'd sooner you went away for he's a very big man and very very fierce.'

'I'm not afraid of him,' said Art, 'what can he do?'

* Indian meal (maize)   † Pigs' trotters

'Well, ' she said, 'he'll ask you a number of riddles. He has to hide for three nights and you have to hide for three nights. . . .'

Before she could finish, or before Art could say whether he was going to stay or go, he heard a deep voice saying: 'Who is this I see in here?' In comes this huge giant and caught poor Art by the throat. 'What are you doing here?' he roared.

'I came to find the heavenly music,' said Art.

'Well, now you've found it,' said the giant, 'and much good may it do you. And I'll tell you something,' he said, 'I'm going to hide for three days and, if you don't find me before the three days are up, I'll cut your head off, skin you, cook you and eat you. And after that,' he roared, 'if you have found me, you'll hide for three days and if I find you, I'll still kill, skin, cook and eat you.'

So poor Art didn't know what to say but, 'Well, I'd like to go back and see to my little stallion.'

'Right,' said the giant, 'but we'll start in the morning.'

'This is an awful thing,' said Art to the stallion when he got back, 'what am I going to do – how do I know where he's going to hide?'

'That's all right,' said the stallion, 'it's getting late at night so we'll want to eat something for, honest to God, my belly thinks my throat is cut. Sit down there now,' said the stallion, 'and put your left hand into my right ear and you'll find a table-cloth. Spread out the table-cloth,' he said, and Art did as he was told. 'Now,' said the stallion, 'put your right hand into my left ear and take out what you'll find there.' Art did that and took out the best of fine food and the finest of old drink. 'Now,' said the stallion, 'you take that for yourself and stick your right hand into my left ear again.' So Art did that and pulled out a bucket of water and a truss of hay. And Art ate the best of fine food and the finest of old drink and the stallion had the hay and the water. 'Now,' said the stallion when they were finished, 'spread yourself out under my legs and we'll go to sleep for the night.' So they went to sleep for the night.

The next morning when they woke up, they could hear the giant shouting: 'Now come and find me if you can.'

'I can tell you where he is,' the little stallion said to Art, 'he's at the top of the tree.' So Art climbed to the top of the tree and there, right enough, was the giant who comes down very highly annoyed. 'Aah!' he roared, 'you found me today, but you won't find me tomorrow.'

After this, Art had great confidence in the stallion; and that night, he again had a feed of the best of fine food and the finest of old drink, and the stallion had a truss of hay and a bucket of clear water, and they carried on a learned discussion until it was time to go to bed.

Next morning when they got up, the stallion said: 'Now go on in through the house and out into the back garden and there you'll see a football. Give the football a good kick.'

'All right,' said Art and off he went and, in the back garden, he gave the football a terrific kick and out spun the giant.

'Well,' said the giant very nastily, 'you got me this time, but you won't get me tomorrow for I've got a trick up my sleeve yet.'

Art went back to the stallion and told him what had happened and said: 'What will we do now?'

'Well,' said the stallion, 'first of all, we'll have a feed.' They ate again all kinds of lovely foods and talked until it was time to go to sleep.

In the morning, Art said: 'What will I do now? Where is he hiding?'

'I'll tell you what to do,' said the stallion. 'When you go inside, ask the girl where he is. But,' he said, 'without the giant understanding you. Just signal to her, where is he?'

So Art goes and sees the daughter of the King of Greece and she is singing away there and he makes signs to ask where is the giant. The girl pointed to a ring on her finger and, at first, Art didn't understand. But she motioned him to take the ring off, which he did. He looked at it and made signs to show that he didn't believe that the giant could fit in such a small ring. But the girl kept singing away and pointed to him to throw it in the fire. So he did that and there was an enormous screech: 'Oh! I'm burnt! I'm burnt!' and out jumped the giant. 'Now,' he roared, 'you caught me the three times, but now it's your turn.'

'All right,' said Art, 'I'll hide tomorrow'.

'Well, now', said Art to the stallion when he went back, 'we're in a right fix now. Where am I going to hide? Sure I'm a stranger here and don't know the place at all.'

'That's all right,' said the stallion, 'I'll tell you in the morning. In the meantime, put your hands in my two ears and take out the grub.' So they had a feed and then Art got under the stallion's legs and slept there for the night.

When he woke up: 'Now,' said the stallion, 'the first thing you do is to take a hair out of my tail and, the hole it leaves, get up into that.' So Art took the hair out of the stallion's tail, got up into the hole and stopped there. And the giant searched all round and couldn't find Art all day and nearly went tearing mad. Art came out that night and the giant said: 'I didn't find you today but I'll find you tomorrow and eat you.'

So that night Art said to the stallion: 'Where am I going to hide tomorrow?'

'That's all right,' said the stallion, 'put your hands into my two ears and take out the food and we'll have a feed first. Then you can stretch out under my legs and have a sleep and we'll talk about the matter in the morning.'

In the morning Art said: 'Now, where am I going to hide?'

'Take a nail out of my hoof,' said the stallion, 'get up into the hole and draw the nail up after you.' So Art did that and stayed there all day, while the giant went round roaring and swearing.

At night, the giant went back to his house and Art came out of the hole and said, 'So you didn't find me'.

'No,' said the giant, 'but I will tomorrow and then I'll kill, skin, cook, and eat you.'

Then Art said to the stallion, 'Where will I hide tomorrow?' and the stallion said: 'One thing at a time. Get out the grub there and we'll have a feed and we'll see about the other matter in the morning.'

'Now,' said the stallion in the morning, when they woke up fresh and early, 'pull out one of my teeth, get up into the hole and draw the tooth up after you.' The giant came rampaging around the place and couldn't find Art and, to cut a long story short, he nearly went demented.

In the evening, Art came out and went into the house and there was the King of Greece's daughter. The music was stopped but she looked happier than ever and she said: 'You have broken the spell. I had to wait for a stranger to come and beat the giant six times.'

'We've done that,' said Art, 'and now I'll take you away from here.'

'All right,' she said, 'although I'm the daughter of the King of Greece.'

'Well,' said Art, 'that's nothing. I'm the King of Ireland's son.' So she jumped up on the back of the stallion behind Art and they rode out of the tunnel and back to his father's palace. The King of Greece's daughter then sang some of the heavenly music for the King of Ireland and the King gave Art half his kingdom. The two brothers were banished and Art and the King of Greece's daughter got married and they had a wedding and everybody ate and drank, and wasn't I at the wedding as well as everybody else and I got a present of a pair of paper boots and a pair of stockings made of buttermilk; and that's the end of my story and all I'm going to tell you.

Landscape near Spiddal, County Galway

Shark-fishing at Achill, County Mayo

Connemara landscape

Westport House, the seat of the Marquis of Sligo

Drumcliff Church

The Confirmation Suit

FOR WEEKS it was nothing but simony and sacrilege, and the sins crying to heaven for vengeance, the big green Catechism in our hands, walking home along the North Circular Road. And after tea, at the back of the brewery wall, with a butt too, to help our wits, what is a pure spirit, and don't kill that, Billser has to get a drag out of it yet, what do I mean by apostate, and hell and heaven and despair and presumption and hope. The big fellows, who were now thirteen and the veterans of last year's Confirmation, frightened us, and said the Bishop would fire us out of the Chapel if we didn't answer his questions, and we'd be left wandering around the streets, in a new suit and top-coat with nothing to show for it, all dressed up and nowhere to go. The big people said not to mind them; they were only getting it up for us, jealous because they were over their Confirmation, and could never make it again. At school we were in a special room to ourselves, for the last few days, and went round, a special class of people. There were worrying times too, that the Bishop would light on you, and you wouldn't be able to answer his questions. Or you might hear the women complaining about the price of boys' clothes.

'Twenty-two and sixpence for tweed, I'd expect a share in the shop for that. I've a good mind to let him go in jersey and pants for that.'

'Quite right, ma'am', says one to another, backing one another up, 'I always say what matter if they are good and pure'. What had that got to do with it, if you had to go into the Chapel in a jersey and pants, and every other kid in a new suit, kid gloves and tan shoes and a scoil* cap. The Cowan brothers were terrified. They were twins, and twelve years old, and every old one in the street seemed to be wishing a jersey and pants on them, and saying their poor mother couldn't be

---

* School

expected to do for two in the one year, and she ought to go down to Sister Monica and tell her to put one back. If it came to that, the Cowans agreed to fight it out, at the back of the brewery wall, whoever got best, the other would be put back.

I wasn't so worried about this. My old fellow was a tradesman, and made money most of the time. Besides, my grandmother, who lived at the top of the next house, was a lady of capernosity and function. She had money and lay in bed all day, drinking porter or malt, and taking pinches of snuff, and talking to the neighbours that would call up to tell her the news of the day. She only left her bed to go down one flight of stairs and visit the lady in the back drawing room, Miss McCann.

Miss McCann worked a sewing-machine, making habits for the dead. Sometimes girls from our quarter got her to make dresses and costumes, but mostly she stuck to the habits. They were a steady line, she said, and you didn't have to be always buying patterns, for the fashions didn't change, not even from summer to winter. They were like a long brown shirt, and a hood attached, that was closed over the person's face before the coffin lid was screwn down. A sort of little banner hung out of one arm, made of the same material, and four silk rosettes in each corner, and in the middle, the letters I.H.S., which mean, Miss McCann said; 'I Have Suffered'.

My grandmother and Miss McCann liked me more than any other kid they knew. I like being liked, and could only admire their taste.

My Aunt Jack, who was my father's aunt as well as mine, sometimes came down from where she lived, up near the Basin, where the water came from before they started getting it from Wicklow. My Aunt Jack said it was much better water, at that. Miss McCann said she ought to be a good judge. For Aunt Jack was funny. She didn't drink porter or malt, or take snuff, and my father said she never thought much about men, either. She was also very strict about washing yourself very often. My grandmother took a bath every year, whether she was dirty or not, but she was in no way bigoted in the washing line in between times.

Aunt Jack made terrible raids on us now and again, to stop snuff and drink, and make my grandmother get up in the morning, and wash herself, and cook meals and take food with them. My grandmother was a gilder by trade, and served her time in one of the best shops in the city, and was getting a man's wages at sixteen. She liked stuff out of the pork butchers, and out of cans, but didn't like boiling potatoes, for she said she was no skivvy, and the chip man was better at it. When she was left alone it was a pleasure to eat with her. She always had cans of lovely things and spicy meat and brawn, and plenty of seasoning, fresh out of the German man's shop up the road. But after a visit from Aunt Jack, she would have to get up and wash for a week, and she would have to go and make stews and boil cabbage and pig's cheeks. Aunt Jack was very much up for sheep's heads too. They were so cheap and nourishing.

But my grandmother only tried it once. She had been a first-class gilder in Eustace Street, but never had anything to do with sheep's heads before. When she took it out of the pot, and laid it on the plate, she and I sat looking at it, in fear and trembling. It was bad enough going into the pot, but with the soup streaming from its eyes, and its big teeth clenched in a very bad temper, it would put the heart crossways in you. My grandmother asked me, in a whisper, if I ever thought sheep could look so vindictive, but that it was more like the head of an old man, and would I for God's sake take it up and throw it out of the window. The sheep kept glaring at us, but I came the far side of it, and rushed over to the window and threw it out in a flash. My grandmother had to drink a Baby Power whiskey, for she wasn't the better of herself.

Afterwards she kept what she called her stock-pot on the gas. A heap of bones, and as she said herself, any old muck that would come in handy, to have boiling there, night and day, on a glimmer. She and I ate happily of cooked ham and California pineapple and sock-eye salmon, and the pot of good nourishing soup was always on the gas even if Aunt Jack came down the chimney, like the Holy Souls at midnight. My grandmother said she didn't begrudge the money for the gas. Not when she remembered the looks that sheep's head was giving her. And all she had to do with the stock-pot was to throw in another sup of water, now and again, and a handful of old rubbish the pork butcher would send over, in the way of lights or bones. My Aunt Jack thought a lot about barley, too, so we had a package of that lying beside the gas, and threw a sprinkle in any time her foot was heard on the stairs. The stock-pot bubbled away on the gas for years after, and only when my grandmother was dead did someone notice it. They tasted it, and spat it out just as quick, and wondered what it was. Some said it was paste, and more that it was gold size, and there were other people and they maintained that it was glue. They all agreed on one thing, that it was dangerous tack to leave lying around, where there might be young children, and in the heel of the reel, it went out the same window as the sheep's head.

Miss McCann told my grandmother not to mind Aunt Jack but to sleep as long as she liked in the morning. They came to an arrangement that Miss McCann would cover the landing and keep an eye out. She would call Aunt Jack in for a minute, and give the signal by banging the grate, letting on to poke the fire, and have a bit of a conversation with Aunt Jack about dresses and costumes, and hats and habits. One of these mornings, and Miss McCann delaying a fighting action, to give my grandmother time to hurl herself out of bed and into her clothes and give her face the rub of a towel, the chat between Miss McCann and Aunt Jack came to my Confirmation suit.

When I made my first Communion, my grandmother dug deep under the mattress, and myself and Aunt Jack were sent round expensive shops, and I came back with a rig that would take the sight of your eye. This time, however, Miss McCann said there wasn't much stirring in the habit line, on account of the mild winter, and she would be delighted to make the suit, if Aunt Jack would get the material. I nearly wept, for terror of what these old women would have me got up in, but I had to let on to be delighted, Miss McCann was so set on it. She asked Aunt Jack did she remember my father's Confirmation suit. He did. He said he would never forget it. They sent him out in a velvet suit, of plum colour, with a lace collar. My blood ran cold when he told me.

The stuff they got for my suit was blue serge, and that was not so bad. They got as far as the pants, and that passed off very civil. You can't do much to a boy's pants, one pair is like the next, though I had to ask them not to trouble themselves putting three little buttons on either side of the legs. The waistcoat was all right, and anyway the coat would cover it. But the coat itself, that was where Aughrim* was lost.

The lapels were little wee things, like what you'd see in pictures like *Ring* magazine of John L. Sullivan, or Gentleman Jim, and the buttons were the size of saucers, or within the bawl of an ass of it, and I nearly cried when I saw them being put on, and ran down to my mother, and begged her to get me any sort of a suit, even a jersey and pants, than have me set up before the people in this get-up. My mother said it was very kind of Aunt Jack and Miss McCann to go to all this

* A battle in 1689 where the Irish were defeated.

trouble and expense, and I was very ungrateful not to appreciate it. My father said that Miss McCann was such a good tailor that people were dying to get into her creations, and her handiwork was to be found in all the best cemeteries. He laughed himself sick at this, and said if it was good enough for him to be sent down to North William Street in plum-coloured velvet and lace, I needn't be getting the needle over a couple of big buttons and little lapels. He asked me not to forget to get up early the morning of my Confirmation, and let him see me, before he went to work: a bit of a laugh started the day well. My mother told him to give over and let me alone, and said she was sure it would be a lovely suit, and that Aunt Jack would never buy poor material, but stuff that would last forever. That nearly finished me altogether, and I ran through the hall up to the corner, fit to cry my eyes out, only I wasn't much of a hand at crying. I went more for cursing, and I cursed all belonging to me, and was hard at it on my father, and wondering why his lace collar hadn't choked him, when I remembered that it was a sin to go on like that, and I going up for Confirmation, and I had to simmer down, and live in fear of the day I'd put on that jacket.

The days passed, and I was fitted and refitted, and every old one in the house came up to look at the suit, and took a pinch of snuff, and a sup out of the jug, and wished me long life and the health to wear and tear it, and they spent that much time viewing it round, back, belly and sides, that Miss McCann hadn't time to make the overcoat, and like an answer to a prayer, I was brought down to Talbot Street, and dressed out in a dinging overcoat, belted, like a grown-up man's. And my shoes and gloves were dear and dandy, and I said to myself that there was no need to let anyone see the suit with its little lapels and big buttons. I could keep the topcoat on all day, in the chapel, and going round afterwards.

The night before Confirmation day, Miss McCann handed over the suit to my mother, and kissed me, and said not to bother thanking her. She would do more than that for me, and she and my grandmother cried and had a drink on the strength of my having grown to be a big fellow, in the space of twelve years, which they didn't seem to consider a great deal of time. My father said to my mother, and I getting bathed before the fire, that since I was born Miss McCann thought the world of me. When my mother was in hospital, she took me into her place till my mother came out, and it near broke her heart to give me back.

In the morning I got up, and Mrs. Rooney in the next room shouted in to my mother that her Liam was still stalling, and not making any move to get out of it, and she thought she was cursed; Christmas or Easter, Communion or Confirmation, it would drive a body into Riddleys, which is the mad part of Grangegorman, and she wondered she wasn't driven out of her mind, and above in the puzzle factory years ago. So she shouted again at Liam to get up, and washed and dressed. And my mother shouted at me, though I was already knotting my tie, but you might as well be out of the world, as out of fashion, and they kept it up like a pair of mad women, until at last Liam and I were ready and he came in to show my mother his clothes. She hanselled him a tanner, which he put in his pocket and Mrs. Rooney called me in to show her my clothes. I just stood at her door, and didn't open my coat, but just grabbed the sixpence out of her hand, and ran up the stairs like the hammers of hell. She shouted at me to hold on a minute, she hadn't seen my suit, but I muttered something about it not being lucky to keep a Bishop waiting, and ran on.

The Church was crowded, boys on one side and the girls on the other, and the altar ablaze with lights and flowers, and a throne for the Bishop to sit on when he wasn't confirming. There was a cheering crowd outside, drums rolled, trumpeters from Jim Larkin's band sounded the Salute. The Bishop came in and the doors were shut. In short order I joined the queue to the rails, knelt and was whispered over, and touched on the cheek. I had my overcoat on the whole time, though it was warm, and I was in a lather of sweat waiting for the hymns and the sermon.

The lights grew brighter and I got warmer, was carried out fainting. But though I didn't mind them loosening my tie, I clenched firmly my overcoat, and nobody saw the jacket with the big buttons and the little lapels. When I went home, I got into bed, and my father said I went into a sickness just as the Bishop was giving us the pledge. He said this was a master stroke, and showed real presence of mind.

Sunday after Sunday, my mother fought over the suit. She said I was a liar and a hypocrite, putting it on for a few minutes every week, and running into Miss McCann's and out again, letting her think I wore it every week-end. In a passionate temper my mother said she would show me up, and tell Miss McCann, and up like a shot with her, for my mother was always slim, and light on her feet as a feather, and in next door. When she came back she said nothing, but sat at the fire looking into it. I didn't really believe she would tell Miss McCann.

And I put on the suit and thought I would go in and tell her I was wearing it this week-night, because I was going to the Queen's with my brothers. I ran next door and upstairs, and every step was more certain and easy that my mother hadn't told her. I ran, shoved in the door, saying: 'Miss Mc., Miss Mc., Rory and Sean and I are going to the Queen's. . . .' She was bent over the sewing-machine and all I could see was the top of her old grey head, and the rest of her shaking with crying, and her arms folded under her head, on a bit of habit where she had been finishing the I.H.S. I ran down the stairs and back into our place, and my mother was sitting at the fire, sad and sorry, but saying nothing.

I needn't have worried about the suit lasting forever. Miss McCann didn't. The next winter was not so mild, and she was whipped before the year was out. At her wake people said how she was in a habit of her own making, and my father said she would look queer in anything else, seeing as she supplied the dead of the whole quarter for forty years, without one complaint from a customer.

At the funeral, I left my topcoat in the carriage and got out and walked in the spills of rain after her coffin. People said I would get my end, but I went on till we reached the graveside, and I stood in my Confirmation suit drenched to the skin. I thought this was the least I could do.

In Connemara

Stiofán O Fláithbheartaigh, Irish folk-singer

Belfast shipyard workers at Harland and Wolff's

4

The Black North

Y E Protestant heroes of Ireland,
Give ear to the words I write down,
Concerning the Aughalee heroes
That marched through the sweet Portadown.

It being the twelfth day of July,
Our music so sweetly did play,
And *The Protestant Boys* and *Boyne Water*
Were the tunes we played marching away.

Like the sons of King William we marched then
Till at length Lurgan Town we did view
Where the church it was there decorated
With the Orange and Purple and Blue.

Round its spires our colours were flying,
Small guns like big cannons did roar.
Long life to those Aughalee heroes
For they are the boys we adore.

Captain Black, like a bold Orange hero,
Came riding down on his grey steed,
And he asked what number we carried
And where we meant for to proceed.

We told him the county of Antrim,
Our number was six-thirty-two,
We are the bold Aughalee heroes
That will soon make the rebels subdue.

We took off our hats to salute him,
As boldly he bade us march on
And he rode like a hero before us
Till we came to the banks of the Bann.

And when we arrived safe in Aughalee,
The brandy did flow like the Rhine,
So long life to those Aughalee heroes,
For they are the boys crossed the Boyne.

Most Northern songs are good ones, though they all seem to be written for brass bands, which is commentary enough on the Conservative Party up there. *The Boyne Water*, *The South Down Militia*, *The Enniskilling Dragoons*, – all have that same imposed militaristic note, even that great song *Lillibulero*, sung by the Derry apprentices after they threw the soldiers of King James back from the walls of Derry. Many a writer has said that the chorus 'Lillibulero bullenala' is incomprehensible gibberish, but this is not the case. At the time of the siege in 1689, the apprentices were Irish-speaking and, defending the Dutch William, their symbol was the Orange lily. The meaning of 'Lillibulero bullenala' is simply *An lile ba léir é – ba linn an lá –* 'the lily was triumphant – we won the day!'

Everybody has heard about the border between the North and South of Ireland but it's not very real in everyday life – you're not going from one country to another. For instance, the B Specials, who are the armed part-time police in the North, drink when they are in the border area on the southern side, rather than on the northern side, for the simple and sufficient reason, that the drink on the southern side is cheaper, and they'd want to be mad if they didn't, and in money matters there are very few Northerners who are off their heads.

I won't say that there's no difference between people north and south of the border, but I will say, without fear of contradiction, that there's less difference between them than there is between, say, a Yorkshire-man and a Somerset man. But you get that strange approach in all countries – every northern part of every country in the world is sup-posed to be sharper than the southern part. The North of France (which is south of the South of England in case you don't know) is supposed to be ferret-eyed and bitter, compared with the South, though if you know the Midi even you wouldn't agree with that; and then again, the North of Italy which is south of the South of France is an industrial area and the people are supposed to be hard, while the southern Italians are supposed to be green and warm-hearted – which indeed they are, but so are the northern Italians. That sort of thing doesn't work at all. Cork is on the south of Ireland and the people have a soft easy-going way about them. The northern people are supposed to be a shrewd people that you wouldn't put anything over on. Yet the deceptively easy-going Corkman would buy – and, what would be far harder, would sell – a Northerner any day of the week without giving it a second thought, and I mean that in no political, but in a severely commercial sense.

The border partitions Ulster more than it does Ireland as a whole. Less than one-fifth of the country is outside the Republic, whereas at least a third of Ulster is outside the jurisdiction of the Northern Government. Three counties of Ireland lie outside this new northern Pale and the people, Protestant or Catholic, are the same people. In several places, the border actually partitions a farmhouse – you could nearly be smuggling whiskey or butter from one room to another without a gauger being any the wiser. Needless to say, that kind of thing is not done, for the people of Ireland, North or South, are too upright and honest to attempt to evade penal taxes for which there is no religious sanction, Protestant or Catholic; so there and sucks to you as the English, in their so disarmingly charming insulting way, are inclined to say.

The working-class areas of Belfast present much the same appearance as the working-class areas in Dublin – unemployed men, wearing the same 'uniform' of caps and chokers – hanging around the same kind of corners and going to the same kind of betting shops. Emigration from the North is about the same as from the South, and despite their much-vaunted industrialism, the rate of unemployment is probably higher than in the South. You have the great sameness of depression in all Irish cities – Belfast, Dublin, Cork, Limerick, Galway – unemployment and emigration, getting to the boat and away, coming home with a few quid, staying happily for a fortnight, miserably for a week, before running back again to some slum in Birmingham, or Wigan or London, where as like as not they sleep four in a bed – two in the day shift and two in the night-shift.

There is very little political difference, in fact, between the two parts of the country. They could swap governments and nobody would notice the change – none of the workers would, at any rate. Their porridge bowls would still be just as they are now – exactly the same amount of porridge would be doled out to them whether the Government was a Dublin or a Belfast one. But I'm convinced that the next forward step in Irish affairs will come from the industrial workers up here, and it is they who will transform Ireland into what the leaders of the 1916 Rising wanted – a Socialist Republic. It should never be forgotten that the people of the North are Irish, not British. There is a nationalist minority of one-third which is wildly against the idea of being British, and there is another two-thirds which is not so much in favour of being British, but are wildly against the idea of being Roman Catholic. Even that two-thirds would be highly insulted if you called them British – except for a small splinter group who have arrived from England in the last twenty years or so.

The middle and upper classes use a show called the Orange Order for keeping the working classes in line. Any time they show signs of getting out of hand and looking for a bigger cut of the joint, some religious issue is raised and the Orange Order calls everyone out for the defence of their ancient freedoms against the imaginary on-slaughts of the Papists. When Lord Randolph Churchill saw the fight in the House of Commons for Irish Home Rule going against him towards the end of the last century, he said, 'We'll play the Orange card'. Off he trots to Belfast and whips up religious feeling there so that, in 1914, when a Home Rule Bill was passed, the Orangemen said that if it was put into effect, they'd fight the King, Lords, Commons, British Army, and anyone else that the British Government cared to put in the ring. When an attempt was then made to send the Army against them, a whole lot of officers refused to obey orders in what was known as the Curragh Mutiny, and the C.I.G.S. was manœuvred into resigning by the Director of Military Operations, Sir Henry Wilson, an Ulsterman who became later the C.I.G.S. To my simple mind, all this looks like treason, but the Orangemen and the generals won and the Home Rule Bill was shelved. But the Orangemen had merely been used in a struggle for power between the Liberals and the Conservatives in England, neither of whom gave a damn about Ireland at all.

It all resulted in the division of Ireland in 1920, under the leadership of a Dublin Unionist named Carson and a Northerner named Craig, later Lord Craigavon. Carson was a bitter little man with an unscrupulous lust for personal power. He had prosecuted Wilde in the eighteen-nineties, and for malevolence and personal viciousness, his cross-examination would take some beating. Craigavon wasn't

Billy Mercer, Belfast Orangeman

so bad. Many years later when he had been Prime Minister for a long time, he said that Ireland was too small to be divided, that partition couldn't last – that unity mightn't come in his lifetime, but come it would have to. There's a story told about him that he went on a cruise once from Belfast during the depression, and his wife said to him as they sailed down Belfast Lough: 'Oh, James, look at the gulls!'

'Nonsense, my dear,' he replied, 'we left them all at home.'

The main Orange turn-out is on the anniversary of the Battle of the Boyne – the twelfth of July. On that day there are processions and bonfires and a mock battle is staged at a place outside Belfast called Scarva. It's a wild day, with lashings of porter flowing like the Boyne itself, and a few people get cracked heads but it's all in fun, as they say. Down the streets of Belfast come all these processions of men with bowler hats, led by fife and drum bands. Everybody wears an Orange sash and you can see the sweat pouring off them as they wallop away at the drums. These are special large drums known as 'Lambegs' and the drummers use canes to beat them with. They keep it up for hours and it is said that a man is not a good drummer unless his knuckles bleed profusely as he keeps on drumming. It's a colourful show, I must admit, and I think when the country is again united, we'll keep it going under the auspices of the Tourist Board – after all, people travel to distant countries to see these tribal ceremonies and dances and, as those up here in the North are as good as any to be found, we might as well make a bit of money out of them.

It's a part of Ireland that lives entirely in the past. Down south, they have had to pay some attention to world affairs – they were in the League of Nations and are well respected for the work they have done since they got into the United Nations; and, of course, it was the South that was mainly responsible for the Statute of Westminster which gave complete independence to Canada, Australia and the other dominions. But the Northern Government has no part to play in the world – they have no power in foreign affairs or in defence or anything like that – it's a kind of superior municipal corporation. The result is that political discussion there is like parish pump politics and, having no power even in social welfare legislation, where they have to tag along after England, they can't look forward but only backwards. There's a good poem by the Belfast poet, Maurice Craig – who left his native city and wrote the best book ever written about Dublin. His poem is called *Ballad to a Traditional Refrain*:

The Boyne Bridge

Red brick in the suburbs, white horse on the wall,
Eyetalian marbles in the City Hall:
O stranger from England, why stand so aghast?
May the Lord in His mercy be kind to Belfast.

This jewel that houses our hopes and our fears
Was knocked up from the swamp in the last hundred years;
But the last shall be first and the first shall be last:
May the Lord in His mercy be kind to Belfast.

We swore by King William there'd never be seen
An All-Irish Parliament at College Green,
So at Stormont we're nailing the flag to the mast:
May the Lord in His mercy be kind to Belfast.

O the bricks they will bleed and the rain it will weep,
And the damp Lagan fog lull the city to sleep;
It's to hell with the future and live on the past:
May the Lord in His mercy be kind to Belfast.

The white horse on the wall refers to the paintings of King Billy on his dashing steed that you see on the side of houses all over the place, but particularly in the Sandy Row area which is a Protestant quarter. In the pubs here, you get the best pint of porter in Ireland, except for the Aran Islands, where it's even better, and the reason is that the Sandy Row men don't stand for any nonsense with their beer. They've actually shot publicans there for not having the booze in the best condition. The Battle of the Boyne that the paintings commemorate, is popularly regarded as a victory over the Pope but, in actual fact, the Pope had a Te Deum sung when he heard of William's victory. The reason was that King James had an alliance with the King of France and the Pope of the day wasn't talking to the King of France – nor to James either. If you tell an Orangeman this, he's likely to insist that the story is just another Fenian invention; but it happens to be the truth.

There's a good pub in Sandy Row, the 'Bluebell,' and a former proprietor refused to allow the Duke of Edinburgh to play the Orange Drum there – on the grounds that he wasn't a member of the Orange Order and that playing the drum was too serious a business for even the Duke to be permitted to do it. A lot of royal visits to the North take place. The Catholic upper and middle class rather fancy them, but they are afraid to say so. The Protestants treat them as a joke, but look on

In the 'Bluebell', Sandy Row

them as a sort of a guarantee that the Six Counties are not going to be handed over to the Republic, for the present, anyhow. The Unionists in the North use the Royal Show as a kind of Conservative Party circus to pull in the votes – just as it does in England. I was never a one for the Show myself, preferring the Victoria Palace to Buckingham Palace.

The Falls Road area is the main Catholic area. I've been there frequently but I remember it mainly for an incident that happened to me round there during the war. I was trying to make an impression on a girl. I was about eighteen, and another fellow and the girl and myself were sitting in a house on the Falls Road drinking tea. The other fellow remarked on the enormous wages being earned by the workers in the shipyard and in the aircraft factory. He referred to one family, in particular, and while I wasn't trying to make the girl think that my people were millionaires, I certainly did not expect him to say: 'And there's the MacSweeneys. Do you know thon crowd, Brendan, have a piano, and before the war, they were the same as ourselves – they had nothing!'

Despite their religious differences, the workers, north and south, are very much the same otherwise. I was talking to a Presbyterian clergyman once out beyond Portrush who had previously ministered down in the South. According to him, the northern people acted much the same as the people in Tipperary, in Kilkenny, in Armagh or anywhere you like to think of. They're not all that notoriously thrifty there in the North and they're very hard drinkers, for instance.

I said to this clergyman: 'Of course, with regard to drink and that, your crowd are not supposed to be as bad as ours.'

'They are,' he said, 'by God, and worse.'

There's more difference between a Manchester man and a London man than there is between a Belfast man and a Dublin man, for instance. On the basis of differences, there'd be more justification for partitioning England.

What causes such difficulties as exist in the North is imposed political discrimination. Religious discrimination just doesn't exist in the South and the authorities of the Protestant churches down there have again and again spoken in the highest terms of the way the minority are treated in all walks of life. The southern Protestants own up to forty per cent of big business and they merge well with the Catholic majority. They don't represent any voting danger, of course, and that's where they differ from the Catholic minority in the North. Up here, the largest single religious group is the Catholic Church –

one-third of the population. They could form a forceful enough opposition if they put their minds to it and, with a higher birth-rate than the Protestants, it's not inconceivable that in our own lifetime, they may form a majority in the Six Counties' area.

On their numbers, they should be entitled to seventeen seats out of fifty-two in the Northern Parliament but, so far as I can recall, they have never succeeded in electing more than twelve. This is due to the gerrymandering of the constituencies by the Unionists, which has the effect that it takes much more votes to elect a Catholic than it does to elect a Unionist. The maximum number of Unionist candidates are elected with the minimum amount of Unionist votes. It's a fiddle and nothing else, and the British should do something about it. They prefer to say, however; 'Oh, partition has nothing to do with us.' They do nothing about it – particularly Conservative Governments – for the sufficient reason that the North sends twelve members to Westminster to bolster up the Conservative Party, as the Unionist Party is a branch of the Conservatives. The Labour Party when it was in power in England, also did nothing about it but for a different reason – the nineteenth-century radical puritanism that informs that party, is much more against Catholicism than against conservatism. So the unfortunate North is caught between the two British parties.

It's this frustrating situation that produces the 'hit-and-run' raids that were going on along the border over the last few years. Most of these were organized from within the Six Counties, in my opinion. It annoyed me, therefore, to hear the northern authorities roaring that the people in the South weren't doing enough to stop the raids – but the incidents occured north of the border, so it stands to reason that northern police weren't doing sufficient to apprehend the men concerned. It suited the authorities in the North to have all these incidents which formed a steady political income for them. It costs a lot of money to keep the B Specials going – one family I used to know had a steady income of £48 a week from the part-time police-work. The expenditure was worth it since, as long as the raids went on, the Unionists' position was consolidated. And the money is still found by the British taxpayer but that's his pleasure – it's no skin off my nose and has nothing to do with me. And so long as the Unionist Party holds on to the Six Counties, the Conservatives have twelve extra votes at Westminster, so really Mr. Macmillan should have sent the raiders a subscription to keep up their work.

Gerrymandering is worse on the local authorities' level and so is

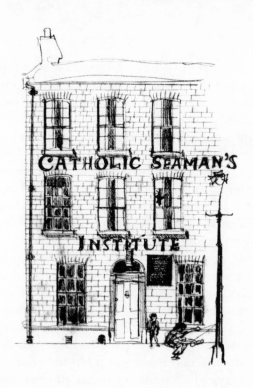

discrimination. Derry has a Catholic nationalist majority but the Derry Corporation is Unionist-controlled, and the same is true in most other areas where the Unionists are in a minority. Discrimination goes on in relation to everything – houses, jobs, and all that. It has frequently happened that ex-servicemen who fought all through the war in the British Forces and were decorated for bravery, don't get jobs once it is found out that they are Catholics. It's very hard for such people to get allocated council houses also. It's mostly the middle classes who practise discrimination. The ordinary Orange working man is like the working man everywhere else – trying to rear his children and hoping that he won't have to get on the next boat to Canada, which is the country that most Northern workers go when they emigrate, rather than to England.

But I remember a friend of mine was taking an English Catholic priest round the North some years ago and explaining to him how Catholics there were subject to intolerance and discrimination. The priest was horrified at the cases that were brought to his attention. One day, they were in this village and the local Catholic Chief Head Man had spent a good deal of time talking about the Protestants and their lack of toleration.

'Tell me,' said the priest, 'how many Protestants have you in this village'.

'One, Father,' said the Head Man, and leaning forward, he tapped the priest on the knee, 'but, with the help of God, we'll have him out by Christmas.'

So you get it on both sides. Another Head Man was explaining the gerrymander in his local council and, on being shown how the constituencies' boundaries were drawn, the priest remarked that it seemed very stupid.

'What's stupid about it?' said the Head Man, '—doesn't it keep them in power?'

Among the younger people, sectarian feeling in the North is tending to die out. A new generation is growing up which, in the middle and upper classes, could be said to be a sort of *New Statesman-Spectator*-reading youth (though I don't think the upper classes read anything other than 'Home Fixtures' and recipes for Irish coffee) and among these people it's beginning to be not quite respectable to be anti-Catholic. At the last election, an Independent Labour man would have been elected in West Belfast, where there is heavy unemployment, if it hadn't been for the intervention of a third, Sinn Fein, candidate.

And Queen's University last year elected a young lady barrister who stood in the Liberal interest and roundly beat the official Unionist candidate. So there's a wind of change up there too that Mr. Macmillan might take note of also.

The Protestant worker, when he's unemployed – which he is frequently – has the British Health Service and other social welfare benefits to fall back on. He can't be blamed for not caring that the Conservative Party opposed all these measures in the British House of Commons, and that it was only against their will that the Unionists at Stormont had to enact them also. He's got the benefits and that's all he gives a damn about just now.

There are people who try to find a little England up north, but they're mostly immigrants – officials who came over in some British Government service and their wives. They refer to 'our little country, Ulster', – they make the mistake of calling the Northerners 'you Irish', they have their Women's Institutes and they listen with great nostalgia to 'Mrs. Dale's Diary' – not that we worry about that or anyone else. My own mother listens to 'Mrs. Dale's Diary' (recently re-named 'The Dales') but she listens rather in the manner of one listening to a programme about the Balubas or the aborigines. The attitude of these people to me is pathetic. On the one hand they regard me as a Southern Irishman and therefore beyond their pale but, on the other hand, they read all about me in the *Sunday Times* and the *Observer* which they regard as 'U' papers, with the result that they don't know what to make of me; but I must say they're very nice about it, though their bewilderment is funny enough.

They are the people, too, who keep calling Derry 'Londonderry'. That's a name that's not used by any indigenous Northerner, not even the Protestants, for they'd be too self-conscious. The right name for the city is Derry from the Irish *Doire Cholm Chille* – meaning the oak-grove of Colmkille. It got the name Londonderry from a company of swindlers that were founded in London, in the seventeenth century, to drive the native Irish off the land and to settle the place with English and Scots.

It's a lovely city, Derry, and the people are all very kind and generous – as they are all over the county. I remember being up there once with my wife and we went out for a picnic. We had cold meat, tomatoes, hard-boiled eggs and bread and butter, but the one thing we needed was a drink, but being Sunday the pubs were shut. I passed a chemist's shop, however, that was open for a couple of hours, and like

many other chemist's shops, there was wine for sale in it. Usually it's Australian Burgundy sold medicinally for the amount of iron in it, for it turns your tongue and teeth black when you drink it. There was an old woman behind the counter and I asked her for a bottle of wine.

'I'm sorry,' she said, 'but it's Sunday and I couldn't sell it. In the first place, it's against the law and in the second place, it would be against my principles, for I'm a teetotaller and I only sell it as medicine.'

'Well, ma'am,' I said, 'it's against my principles to drink anything else but wine. I'm not a Presbyterian but a Calathumpian'.

'Oh!' she said, 'I never heard of them. What are they?'

'Well,' I said, 'they're a religion that would sooner eat the stalks of cabbage than the leaves. But another important part of our faith is founded strictly on the Bible and, as a good Presbyterian, you know that wine was almost the only thing they drank in Biblical times.'

'What,' said she, 'about milk?'

'It interferes with my digestion,' I said; 'I'd be going against my doctor's orders if I drank milk, and I'd be going against my religion if

I drank tea or coffee, and I'm just about to have something to eat and I need something to drink with my food.'

'Well,' she said then, 'I won't interfere with any man's covenant with God for the sake of any man-made law,' and she gave me the bottle of wine, which was drunk by my wife and myself with humility and pious gratitude.

The rural parts of the North are very beautiful but, being a city man myself, I prefer Belfast to the country outside it. And partly the reason for my fondness for that Manchester-like city is that it is the heart of proletarian Ireland. It will be the Belfast worker who will upset both the green and the orange apple-carts, so in his honour I'll sing him a rebel song from the North, to while away the time as we await the Rising there:

> Oh! see the fleet-foot hosts of men who speed with faces wan
> From farmstead and from fisher's cot upon the banks of Bann.
> They come with vengeance in their eyes, too late, too late are they,
> For Roddy McCorley goes to die on the Bridge of Toome today.
>
> Up the narrow street he stepped, smiling and proud and young,
> About the hemp-rope on his neck, the golden ringlets clung.
> There's never a tear in the blue, blue eyes; both glad and bright are they,
> As Roddy McCorley goes to die on the Bridge of Toome today.
>
> Oh! when he at last stepped up that street, his shining pike in hand,
> Behind him marched in grim array, a stalwart earnest band.
> For Antrim town! For Antrim town! He led them to the fray,
> Now Roddy McCorley goes to die on the bridge of Toome today.
>
> The grey coat and its sash of green were brave and stainless then.
> A banner flashed beneath the sun over the marching men.
> The coat hath many a rent this noon, the sash is torn away,
> As Roddy McCorley goes to die on the Bridge of Toome today.
>
> Because he loved the motherland, because he loved the green,
> He goes to meet the martyr's fate with proud and joyous mien,
> True to the last! True to the last! He treads the upward way,
> Young Roddy McCorley goes to die on the bridge of Toome today.
>
> O Ireland, mother Ireland, you love them still the best, -
> The fearless few who fighting fall upon your hapless breast.
> But never a one of all your dead, more bravely fell in fray
> Than he who marches to his fate on the bridge of Toome today.

Derry: the City Walls

Honour Ireland's Dead
Remember 1916

Off the Falls Road, Belfast

Belfast: in the Sandy Row district

The Variety Market, Belfast

Tommy Kelly, barman at the 'Bee',
Falls Road, Belfast

A COUPLE OF QUICK ONES

Buíochas do James Joyce

Annseo i Rue St. Andre des Arts
i dtabhairne Arabach, ólta,
miním do Fhranncach fiosrach thú
Ex-G.I.'s 's Rúiseach ólta.
Molaim gach comhartha dár chuiris ar phár
Is mise san Fhrainc ag ól Pernod dá bharr.
Maidir le conteur is bródúil sinn díot
Is buíoch den Chalvados ólaimíd tríot.

Da mba mise tusa
Is tusa mé féin
Ag teacht ó Les Halles
Is ag iompar an méid seo cognac
Ag seinnt ar lánbholg
Scríofá-sa bhéarsa nó dhó do mo mholadh.

Thanks to James Joyce

Here in the rue St. Andre des Arts
In an Arab tavern, pissed,
For a studious Frenchman I construe you,
Ex. G.I.'s and a Russian, pissed.
All of those things you penned I praise
While, in France, I swill Pernod in return:
Proud of you as a writer we are
And grateful for the Calvados we owe to you.

If you were me
And I were you
Leaving Les Halles
Holding all this cognac,
On a full belly bawling,
You'd write a verse or two in my praise.

Oscar Wilde

Do Seán Ó Súilleabháin

Oscar Wilde, Poète et Dramaturge,
né à Dublin le 15 Octobre, 1856,
est mort dans cette maison
le 30 Novembre, 1900

Tréis gach gleo
Do chuir sé as beo
le teann anaithe
sínte sa chlapsholus
corpán an bheomhaire
balbh san dorchadas.
Fé thost, ach coinnle
an tórraimh na lasracha.
A cholainn sheang
's a shúil daingean ídithe
i seomra fuar lom
's an concierge spídeach
o an-iomarca freastail
ar phótaire iasachta
a d'imthigh gan service
. an deich fén gcéad íoctha.
Aistrithe ón Flore
do fhásach na naomhthach',
ógphrionnsa na bpeacadh
ina shearbhán aosta,
seod órdha na drúise
ina dhiaidh aige fágtha,
gan Pernod ina chabhair aige
ach uisge na cráifeacht'.
Ógrí na háilleacht'
ina Narcissus briste,
ach réalt na glanmhaighdine
ina ga ar an uisge

Ceangal

Dá aoibhne bealach an pheacaidh
is mairg bás gan beannacht
Mo ghraidhn thú, a Oscair,
bhí sé agat gach bealach.

Oscar Wilde

For Sean O'Sullivan

Oscar Wilde, Poète et Dramaturge,
né à Dublin le 15 Octobre, 1856,
est mort dans cette maison
le 30 Novembre, 1900.

After all the strife,
That, alive, he caused,
Ravaged with fear,
In the half-light stretched,
The gay spark's body
Lies dumb in the dark,
Silent, the funereal
Candles guttering.
The graceful body,
The firm gaze, spent
In a cold bare room
With a concierge spiteful
From too much attendance
On a foreign tippler
Who left without paying
The ten per cent service.
Exiled from the Flore
To a saintly desert,
The young prince of sin
A withered churl,
The gold jewel of lust
Left far behind him,
No Pernod to brace him
Only holy water,
The young king of Beauty
A ravished Narcissus
As the star of the pure Virgin
Glows on the water

Envoi

Delightful the path of sin
But a holy death's a habit.
Good man yourself there, Oscar,
Every way you had it.

[181]

Donegal landscape

Belfast: at the Market

The Gardens at Powerscourt

5

Epilogue
Appointed to be Read in Churches

JAMES JOYCE was forever referring to Hadrian the Fourth, the only English Pope, a man called Nicholas Breakspear. It was he who gave Henry II a Bull authorizing him to go and impose some discipline on the Catholic Church in Ireland. The Church in Ireland has always tended to be somewhat independent of Rome. The granting of the Bull was ironic, as it was the Irish that converted the English and Scots to Christianity. The Bishops decided to give fealty to their liege, Henry II, and all down the centuries they have tended to side with the English authority. Although Elizabeth I was against Catholicism, the Archbishop of Armagh at the time sided openly with the Elizabethan troops that were ravishing the country. Again in 1798, the Catholic Archbishop of Dublin ordered prayers to be said for the defeat of the rebels. A lot of Presbyterian clergymen took part in that uprising and a number of Catholic priests, notably Father Murphy, in Wexford, who was goaded into supporting his flock by the atrocities of the yeomen – a sort of militia organized from among the sons of wealthy Episcopalian farmers. He fought bravely against them and against the Hessians, the German troops employed to crush the rebellion. Even to this day, it's an insult to be called a Hessian in some parts of Ireland. Most people don't know that the term means a native of Hesse – they think it's some kind of a monster. Father Murphy was excommunicated, but now he's regarded by the Church as a martyr for faith and fatherland.

The greatest disaster to happen to any one nation in Europe, until the murder of six million Jews in the last war, was the Irish Famine of

[185]

1847. Eight million people lived in Ireland at the time, but when the famine ended there were only four million left. I heard an old woman myself, when I was a child of six, tell how she saw a woman on the side of the road at Santry, outside Dublin, with the green juice of the grass running down her lips and a child tugging at her dead breasts. These are things that are not forgotten in a generation. Maybe they say that we Irish have long memories but the Famine is not the kind of thing that can be forgotten in a day or a year.

The English story is that the potato failed and that the Irish depended on the potato as nothing else was grown in Ireland. In fact, Ireland exported more than enough corn and beef in 1847 to feed her population four times over. The food had to be sold for rent to keep the landlord and his wife and mistresses in comfort in England. All of the nations sent shiploads of food to relieve the Irish then, but they were not allowed to land for the simple reason that the policy of the Government was that the Irish should be exterminated. The *Morning Post* said that: 'The Celt is going, going with a vengeance. Very shortly an Irishman will be as scarce on the banks of the Shannon as an Indian on the banks of Potomac.' But I'm happy to report that the *Morning Post* is gone and, by Jesus, we're here yet. The Bishop of Kildare and Leighlin, who was known as J.K.L., said that he was proud that the people of his diocese were so God-fearing that they would sooner die of starvation than refuse to pay the rent. Well, die they did, and they weren't helped much by Government or Church. Queen Victoria was very distressed at the famine among her loyal subjects and she sent £5 to the Famine Relief Fund; then in case she might be thought to be showing open sympathy with a crowd of rebels, she sent £5 to the Battersea Dogs' Home.

At the time of the Fenian Movement, Dr. Moriarty, the Bishop of Kerry, declared that Hell wasn't hot enough, nor Eternity long enough, to punish the Fenians. The Church always preferred British occupation and British patronage than to side with, and take a chance with, their own devoted Catholic flock. Later, when the Land League was formed to fight against the big land-owners and to support the small farmer, they were against that. When the farmers united and refused to occupy the land of an evicted tenant – a programme known as 'the Plan of Campaign' – the Pope was persuaded to declare such behaviour a mortal sin. So that the Irish, who received so few privileges from the Catholic Church, did receive the privilege of having a new mortal sin instituted on their behalf.

The Church sided with the hypocrite Gladstone against Parnell, and later in 1920 the Catholic Bishop of Cork of the time, declared that any person attacking a Black and Tan was guilty of murder – that the Black and Tans were the lawful forces of the Crown and, as such, were entitled to the respect and assistance of the population. The night after he made this pronouncement, six young men were butchered with hatchets by the Black and Tans in County Cork. In 1922, the Church excommunicated Mr. De Valera and Mr. Sean T. O'Kelly, both subsequently decorated by the Pope. In my own time, the I.R.A. prisoners in England in 1939 were grossly treated by the clergy there.

A lot of the ordinary priests in the country were very good. Working close to their flock, they knew the hardships and the difficulties and sympathized with them. Two great priests, Father Albert and Father Dominick, a Capuchin and a Dominican, were exiled out to California and Cuba because they had identified themselves with the people's cause from 1916 to 1922. And you get isolated incidents that show the Church's bias even today. A few years ago in a corporation housing scheme in Co. Dublin, a co-operative society was formed by the local housewives to buy food for themselves as cheaply as they could get it. The local shop-keepers rose up in arms against the co-operative, and the local clergy supported them and denounced it as communistic and succeeded in smashing it.

Some years ago, a football match was played in Dublin between Ireland and Yugoslavia and the Archbishop of Dublin said nobody should go to it because it was against a Communist country. All the same, the then Minister for Justice, himself a former footballer, and 33,000 other Dublin people, turned up to see it.

I met a priest friend of mine at the match and he said to me: 'Brendan, is Yugoslavia a Communist country?'

'Well,' I answered, 'I don't know. One of my brothers who is not a Communist says that it is; but, on the other hand, another brother, who is a Communist, says that it is not. All in all,' I said, 'as you're here, you'd better take my Stalinist brother's view that it's not.'

Which reminds me of the priest in Galway who was talking to myself and some English tourists and one of the tourists asked him: 'Do you believe in the hereafter, Padre'?

The barman dropped a glass and said: 'Well, be Christ, well, if he doesn't believe in the hereafter, it's a pretty poor look out for the rest of us.'

The Protestant Church in Ireland has been worse. Their history consists entirely of backing up the landlords, which maybe was natural enough as they were both minorities. They still have enormous properties in the country from which they draw great rents. But it would be a great mistake to think that in Ireland the Protestant Churches were in any way progressive – they were not. The greatest Irish patriots down to quite recent times were Protestants – Wolfe Tone, Robert Emmet, Lord Edward Fitzgerald, the brothers Sheares, Thomas Davis, John Mitchell and others – but even today, with the advent of national independence, the Protestant Church doesn't go out of its way to make much of them. Until quite recently, too, – and even now for all I know – Protestant services used to close with prayers for the British monarch, which seems a bit dated and out of touch with 'an important phase of reality', to use a phrase of Conor Cruise O'Brien's.

The Jews have always been close to the people and respected, like the Quakers. Both make a lot of money but good luck to them – they're on the whole good employers. I was serving a sentence during the war in Ireland for attempting to murder two policemen – who weren't charged with a prior attempt to murder me – and I was in for fourteen years though I was amnestied in 1948. But I remember that it was the Quakers who used to send us in draught games, ludo games and other little odds and ends like that, that helped to pass the time. Only one other organization looked after us. That was the Clan na Gael in America, who sent us quantities of a terrible tobacco, the name of which I forget. The late Joe McCarthy tried to become a member of the Clan at one time in his game, but they weren't having any, so his attempt to become an Irish patriot also fizzled out.

It is funny how nations come in and out of fashion. The Irish had a great vogue before the First World War, but when they started looking for independence they got the knock. The Jews came into fashion during the Hitler régime, when every decent person leaned over backwards to support them. The Scots had their go even before the Irish. They were very popular in the time of the late Queen Victoria, who wrote a book about them called *Leaves from My Diary in the Highlands*. It was translated into Scots Gaelic. I don't know what was in it, but when the Dean of Windsor heard she was going to produce another one, he went to work and persuaded her not to. She hardly ever spoke to him again. She had a friend called John Brown and she put up a lot of statues to him that all had to be knocked down after her death.

There was an old Fenian who was in prison in Mountjoy who said that he always smoked duty-free tobacco and he'd never use goods on which duty had been paid to Mrs. Brown – Queen Victoria. His name was Pagan O'Leary, and he got the nick-name because when he was asked in prison what his religion was, he said 'I'm an old Milesian pagan.'

'Sorry, mate,' they said, 'if you come in here you've got to be either a Protestant or a Catholic.'

'Very well,' he said, 'put me down a Catholic. I'd prefer to be a beggar than a thief.'

Shortly afterwards, someone asked in the House of Commons if it was true that, while in prison, Pagan O'Leary was being compelled to dis-practise his religion!

There always has been a certain amount of anti-clericalism in Ireland, though it seldom goes as far as Pagan O'Leary. It's the Church's own fault for always being against the people's political inclinations towards independence. The only instance I recall where the Church did support the people, was at the time of the anti-conscription campaign in 1918. I always liked the story about the great Prince Gerald of the fifteenth or sixteenth century who fought nobly against the English – he was an ancestor of the present Duke of Leinster. He burnt the cathedral at Kildare and, when asked why he did it, he answered, 'Honest to God, I wouldn't have done it, only I thought the Archbishop was in it.'

They're responsible for most reaction in Ireland. The Church I mean. The censorship of books, of plays – both official and unofficial censorship – and they oppose progressive legislation, the most recent instances being when they opposed the institution of a free mother-and-child medical care scheme in 1951, and when they opposed any kind of adoption legislation – though this was eventually accepted in 1952 or thereabouts.

Even in times gone by, a fair amount of satire was written on the clergy by the poets. Here, in translation, are a few epigrams that will illustrate what I mean:

> The monks are upright people
> They are usually very pleasant.
> If churlishness goes with holiness,
> Then the priests are saints.

*

If you desire the monks' goodwill,
Go with them as you ought.
Give them all they ask
But ask them for naught.

*

When the whale swims in the Main
When France is on Slieve Mish,
When the priests loose their greed,
Then shall the crow sing sweetly.

There's no point in attacking the Church nowadays for the old reasons that it was anti-nationalist. Things have changed since most of the young priests grew up in an independent Ireland and are themselves Irish-speaking and national-minded. But one doesn't forget the clergy's history when you find them opposing social progress – entering into an alliance with doctors against nationalized medicine – and that sort of thing. Actually, nowadays, the average parish priest and curate is a jovial, intelligent and, on the whole, good-natured person and, in his attitude to land ownership and land division, much more progressive than their Protestant colleagues.

Northern Ireland, in fact, where the Protestants have a majority, is much more feudal than the South. There are still huge estates up there where the loyal tenantry come out and light bonfires for the young master's twenty-first birthday. The North is one of the last redoubts of flunkeyism in these islands – the British Isles, as they are generally called – though the Department of External Affairs in Dublin tries to popularize the term 'West European Islands'. It doesn't matter a damn what they're called, they're entirely surrounded by water, and anyway the early Britons, like Boadicea, were Celts and their language was much closer to Irish than to English.

Such differences as exist between Britain and Ireland nowadays, are due more to economics and to social environment than to racial characteristics. The two nations are inextricably mixed up and little in the way of national characteristics divide them. If you go into a pub in Manchester, Belfast, Dublin, Liverpool, or London, you will hear people sing one song which might almost be their National Anthem: *I've got a lovely bunch of coconuts*, and their second favourite is *Nellie Dean*. My sister, for instance, lives in Crawley, a new town in Sussex, and she's much more interested in the problems of the woman next door who is probably about the same age, has the same number of babies, and the same difficulties in making her husband's pay last from one Friday to the next, than she is in the differences between the English and the Irish.

We have, of course, a different language and that's one thing that the English are inclined to look askance at – though it's no skin off their nose. I'm in favour of compulsory Irish as a school subject – it's no burden to learn it and, indeed, I regard it as important. Stalin, in his day, said a number of sensible things and I think it was he who said that 'language is the memory of a people'. Apart from that, the Irish language is so inextricably mixed up with the English spoken in Ireland, that it's practically a necessity to learn it if you want to know what you're saying! And that goes for the North, too, for in living memory Irish was the daily language in the glens of Antrim.

One thing the Northerner shares with the Southerner is a narrow-mindedness in matters of sex and religion, and conversation on either of these subjects is frowned upon. Both North and South are convinced that Providence has erected a wall to keep out the devils of sexual immorality and a roof to keep out the nuclear bomb. Both of these conceits are good in their own way and certainly not to be too much condemned. Ireland, after all, is not a piece of America, nor yet a piece of England. It's a different place and I'll say this for it, it's very liberal-minded in drinking matters, which is more than can be said for England, and nobody cares what you wear or where – though I did hear that the Bishop of Galway last year spoke about girls walking through the streets of Galway in shorts – but that's very unusual, even for a Bishop.

I was trudging up the road from Salthill in Galway myself one hot summer's day, and the beautiful strand of Spiddal lay within a few feet of me, with the Atlantic inviting me into its smoothness and coolness. I took off my clothes and ran into the water, lay and regarded my naked form in comfort and at my ease. I was suddenly brought back to reality by the shouts of a number of young men and women making their way to the water's edge; and I realized that I had no togs on and how was I to get out? The nearest laundry consonant with modesty was on the East Coast of the United States. Suddenly I recognized some voices and I found that who was it coming down for a late swim but the Abbey Players who were on holiday in Spiddal. I swam towards them, shouted out a greeting, and ran up the beach as fast as I could to where my clothes were, and I dried and dressed myself. Then we all retired to a very pleasant pub and we spent the evening singing, drinking, dancing and generally diverting ourselves. Somebody remarked on the fact that I had had no clothing on when I got out of the water earlier on, and I said: 'No, but I didn't mind; for one half of you is men and the other half is actresses.'

So there you are. Ireland is like that – a land of contrasts like every other country – rigid in some matters, free and easy in others. You can take it or leave it, and that's the end of my story and all I am going to tell you and thanks for coming along.